SURVIVAL
SCRAPBOOK 2.

SCHOCKEN BOOKS • NEW YORK

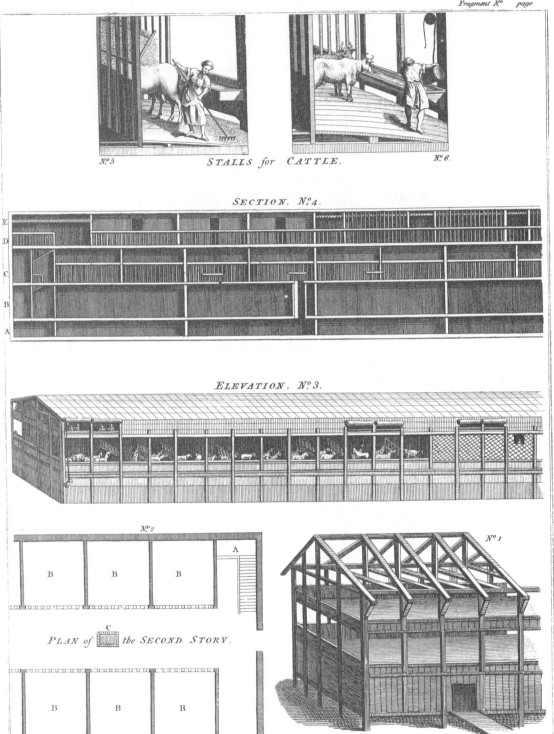

Nᵒ5   STALLS for CATTLE.   Nᵒ6.

SECTION. Nᵒ4.

ELEVATION. Nᵒ3.

Nᵒ2   Nᵒ1

PLAN of the SECOND STORY.

CONSTRUCTION of NOAH'S ARK.

First SCHOCKEN EDITION 1973

Published in cooperation with Unicorn Bookshop   Brighton/Seattle

Library of Congress Catalog Card No. 73-82211

Copyright©1972 Stefan A. Szczelkun

Manufactured in the United States of America

Second Printing, 1974

ARK

INFORMATION AREA	INFORMATION UNIT

forward facing.....back facing

TITLE.....................ARK
CONTENT ....CONTENT
INTRODUCTION...........MAZE.

NUTRITION..................SELECTION
5 NUTRIENTS............5 NUTRIENTS
FLESH........................PLANT
VEGETARIAN?.............YIN YANG

AIR.........................BREATHIN1234.

WATER.......................CYCLE
FINDING WATER.........PURIFICATION
COLLECTION................WELLS
PUMPS.......................STORAGE

GROWTH......................GROWING SCRAPS
CHART.........................SELF SUBSISTENCE
COMPOST.....................PEST CONTROL
MUSHROOMS................HYDROPONICS

GATHERING...................STAFF & STAPLE
WILD FOOD 1.................WILD FOOD 2.
WILD FOOD 3.................WILD FOOD 4.
WILD FOOD 5.................WILD FOOD 6.
WILD FOOD 7.................DISINTEGRATED FARM

REARIN ANIMALS.............MILKERS
RABBITS & POULTRY.........BEE & PIG
PISCICULTURE................FISH FARMING

HUNTING.....................LEGAL
VERMIN AS FOOD..........TRAP
CATAPULT....................FISHING 1.
FISHING 2...................FISH BAIT
SPECIES......................PONDS

INFORMATION AREA	INFORMATION UNIT	
	forward facing	back facing
	PROCESS.....................BUYING TOWNS.....................PRESERVING 1. PRESERVING 2..............SYNTHESIS COOKING....................RECIPES	
	WASTE?.....................PIT PRIVY AQUA PRIVY................EARTH CHEMICAL...................SEPTIC TANK MISCELLANEOUS..........WASTE NOT	
	BIBLIOGRAPHY ONE..........BIBLIOGRAPHY TWO BIBLIOGRAPHY THREE.......BIBLIOGRAPHY FOUR BIBLIOGRAPHY FIVE..........BIBLIOGRAPHY SIX BIBLIOGRAPHY SEVEN.......BIBLIOGRAPHY EIGHT	

CONTENT

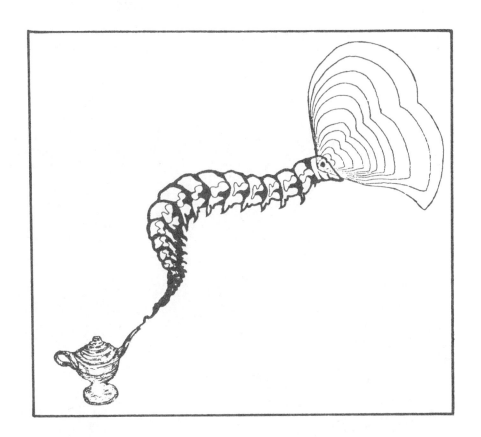

VEGETABLE growing can involve the 'greenest' gardener with the cosmic and biological cycles of which we are a part.

One acre of land can easily be made to produce food for a family of five to ten people, but if intensive techniques are used, five people may live off as little as a quarter of an acre.

It is becoming increasingly difficult to obtain good cheap food — the best method of getting unadulterated food, is to grow it organically yourself.

One acre of land (about 50 × 100 yards) can cost as little as £100 in rural areas, but within 50 miles of London the price increases to £250 per acre. Towns always have allotments, which can be rented for nominal sums of less than £1. Gardens in cities are often unused waste areas ~ perhaps you can dig your friend's!

Without any money at all, you can farm waste land or learn to live by gathering, hunting and scavenging ~.

OUR nutritional requirements are obtained through
the combination and interaction of a great many
substances which are available in common foods.
A balanced diet is important, rather than the
measured intake of any particular essential nutrient.
Each body, activity, time and place has its own
requirement within the broadly known framework
of nutritional knowledge. If your body is to work
well then you must discover the best diet for your
own mind and body by careful experiment and
acute observation of the effects of various foods.

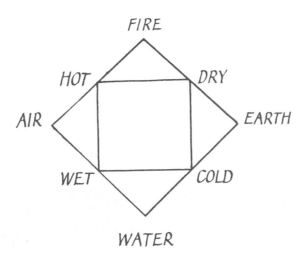

This Alchemically derived diagram governed
much early western food choice and its supposed
effect on health. The idea being that of balancing
one characteristic against another ⎯⎯

In a survival situation, food
is not the immediate priority;
and is best left alone if water
is not available as it will use
up water. This is particularly
true of proteins which need
more water than carbohydrates.
Remember, you can _exist_ for at
least 28 days or longer without
any food.

The R.A.F. survival school sug-
gest that almost anything that
walks, crawls, swims or flies
can be eaten. This includes
snakes, worms, ants, eggs,
shellfish, slugs, lizards,
frogs (not toads), squirrels,
crickets, rats, termites,
grass hoppers, seagulls and
thousands of other animals not
normally considered as food by
Western man.

Most wild plants are edible,
and the liklihood of being fat-
ally poisoned is small, but in
a survival situation be over-
cautious. Vomiting, caused by
the stomach reacting to things
it is not used to will weaken
you considerably. Grass, ferns,
inner tree bark, seaweeds (not
threadlike ones), plankton, are all
examples of food plants not normally considered as such.

Test for Plant Edibility

1. Avoid unknown plants that are
brilliantly coloured, have a
milky sap or bitter taste and
all fungi if no thorough knowledge.
2. Bite off a small test
piece.
3. Keep this piece inside the
lower lip for five minutes.
4. If there is no soapy/bitter/
acid/burning after this time,
swallow.
5. Wait for at least 2 hours
and it is best to wait 10.
6. Gradually increase the dose,
but go steady for the first 24
hours,
7. If no ill effects after the
24 hours, the plant is safe.

Fish Often the easiest creatures to catch, but beware of
fish with flabby skin, slimy
gills, hard scales, small
mouths, evil looking spines,
round or box shaped bodies
and deep set eyes. Don't eat
fish that stinks. Beware if
dent from pressed in thumb
stays in. Also leave black
mussels, sea snakes, long tailed
rays, jelly fish. Surface fish
in open water are safest. Cooking fish improves digestibility
and reduces possibility of the
civilised stomach reacting.

SELECTION

Schizymenia edulis.
(Dulse)

HELIX POMATIA.

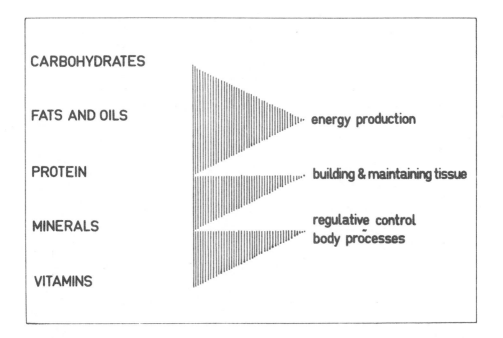

CARBOHYDRATES

FATS AND OILS   energy production

PROTEIN   building & maintaining tissue

MINERALS   regulative control
                                                      body processes

VITAMINS

The human body is composed of 44 elements. 28 of these are only present in minute quantities and are known as trace elements usually having particular functions to play. The other 16 principal elements make up the main fabric of the body.

All the body functions need energy and this is provided by the oxidation of carbohydrate or fats.

ENERGY NEEDED DAILY	CALORIES
Hard physical work	4000
Mod. physical work	3500
Light muscular work	3000
Office work	2500
In bed	1800

Carbohydrates are present in all "starchy" foods, such as cereals, roots and sugars. Carbohydrates when they are digested are converted into glucose which circulates through the body in the blood stream. It is this blood glucose which is the body's energy source.

Fats and oils have twice the energy value of carbohydrates for a given weight, and are present in both animals and vegetables. Animals use fat for insulation and energy storage. Fats are emulsified within the intestine and broken into its constituent parts of glycerol plus fatty acid, in which form they enter the bloodstream. Fats are composed of carbon, hydrogen and oxygen but combined in different proportions to carbohydrates.

5 NUTRIENTS

FOOD	Protein	Carbohydrate	Fat	Calorie per ounce
Milk..................	1	1.5	1	20
Butter................	0	0	25	225
Cheese (cheddar).....	8	0	10	120
Margarine............	0	0	23	220
Eggs.................	3.5	0	3.5	45
Beef.................	4	0	8	90
Bacon................	4	0	11	120
Chicken..............	6	0	2	45
Cod..................	4.7	0	0	19
Eel..................	5.3	0	2.6	46
Mackerel.............	5.3	0	2	40
Salmon...........	6.2	0	3.6	60
Bread, white.........	2	15	0.4	70
Wholemeal............	2.3	13	0.6	65
Oatmeal..............	4.0	18	2	110
Rice.................	2	24	0.3	100
Haricot beans........	6	13	0	73
Peas.................	1.5	4.7	0	26
Sugar (refined)...... ..	0	28	0	116
Potato...............	0.6	6	0	25
Green vegetable......	0.8	1	0	6 approx.
Roots...............	0.4	2	0	10 value
Fruits...............	0.3	3	0	20 only

PROTEIN

Protein is the name not of a
single compound but a group,
each member of which has a
different chemical composition. The nine essential Amino
acids, which are the substances known under the heading of
protein were recognised and
isolated between 1820 and 1935.
It was in 1879 that it was
discovered that the value of
protein depended on the app-
ropriate combination of amino
acids. An egg is considered
to have an "ideal" amino acid
balance for nutrition (although
it has other nutritional dis-
advantages), followed by meat,
- oats and milk - rice and fish.
Pulses, nuts, fungi and green
leaves also contain protein although the range of amino acids
is not so balanced. Protein is
broken down to the amino acid
during digestion. The amino
acids are used for general body
building, repair and maintenance,
A "normal" adult requirement is
about 60 gms. per day - over
consumption not being good. It
is claimed by some dieticians,
that on a mineral rich diet it
is possible to reach a nitrogen
balance on a protein consumption
as low as 35 gms. per day.

VITAMINS

Until 1920 the only components
of food apart from protein, fat
and carbohydrate that were known
were some of the mineral salts.
Before this, vitamins were completely unknown. Vitamins cat-
alyse, control and regulate
body functions and are found
abundantly in green leaves,
milk, eggs, fruits, and generally whole foods are richer
in vitamins than processed.

VITAMINS WE KNOW OF

1. Vitamin A	8. Biotin
2. Beta Carotene	9. Vit B.12
3. Thiamine	10. Ascorbic acid
4. Riboflavin	11. Vit D
5. Niacin	12. Vit E
6. Pontothenic Acid	13. Vit K
7. Pryidoxin	14. Folacin

Mineral Salts

Salts of Calcium, Iron, phospher-
ous, sulphur, magnesium, iodine,
sodium, potassium, cobalt, copper,
manganese, florine, zinc, moly-
bdenum are among the necessary
salts available in foodstuff and
necessary for the healthy running of the body. Calcium, pho-
sphorous and iron are considered to be the most important.

It should be emphasised here
that the food requirements although now broadly classified
are still not known to any great
extent. For instance within the
group known as carbohydrates,
there may be substances with
functions other than purely fuel.

SOME NOTES ON COMMON FOOD GROUPS

MEAT

Generally meat contains fat, protein, glycogen and vitamins in the A and B group, but the composition of meat and its food value depends on the animal species and its age. A young animal will have less lean meat and fat in proportion to bone and fibre than the adult. It is important that an animal is fed well during its youth or the head and bones will develop at the expense of the fleshy parts. The properties of animals and thus the quality and amount of meat may be improved by selective breeding and it is for this reason that meat producing animals are bred with short legs.

The colour of an animal's fat, the amount of which varies at different parts of the carcass is an indication of its age and feeding habits. In general dark fat = old animals. Colour of muscle also indicates the animals' history in that dark flesh contains more haemoglobin from being more vigorously exercised. Confined animals generally will have paler flesh than a free ranging or wild animal of the same species. These variations affect the flavour of meat.

Chicken, duck, venison and reindeer have the highest percentage of protein. Liver has a higher concentration of vitamins and some minerals as it is the main storage organ of the body. Liver, heart, brains and kidney contain significant amounts of Vitamin C or ascorbic acid.

Meat from an animal that has been well fed and rested is higher in preserving acid than meat from frightened, hungry or exercised animals, which tend also to have aesthetically unpleasants taints; so it is better to kill animals instantly when they are calm, rather than frightening them or allowing them to run or struggle.

FISH

The food value of fish meat is high, but it varies with the physiological state, the most important factor of which is the sexual state of the fish. This may affect taste considerably. Fish go "off" comparitively quickly because of a substance called trimethylameoxide which is quickly broken down by bacterial action.

ANIMAL PRODUCE

Milk and dairy. Milk is not the perfect food sometimes imagined, for other than infants at a particular stage in their life. It also has the nutritional disadvantage of containing cholesterol, animal fats and strontium 90, particularly evident for those leading sedentary lives.

Eggs. The modern hen is a highly specialised biological machine for the concentration and conversion of raw food materials. The hen which lays between 200-300 eggs per year has been developed from the jungle fowl which lays only 20-25 eggs per year.
The egg is almost perfect protein food except for the disadvantage again of containing cholesterol which can be harmful if many eggs are eaten regularly. Raw eggs also contain avidin which is capable of inducing vitamin deficiency.

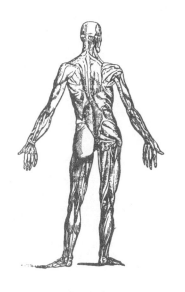

FLESH

CEREALS contain a wide range of
nutrients, and it is apt to men-
tion what they lack rather than
what they contain. Generally,
they are deficient in Vitamins A
and D and the relative amounts of
amino acids is less satisfactory
than those found in animal foods;
particularly a deficiency of the
amino acid lysine. When completely dried, none of them will
contain Vitamin C.

Wheat is our most widely known
cereal, growing best in temper-
ate regions with 13-35" of rainfall per year. Barley, oats and
rye grow in similar conditions,
but are not as suitable as wheat
for baking bread. Rice is exten-
sively grown in warmer, humid
climates being the staple diet
of a large proportion of the
human race.

All cereals will contain more
vitamins and minerals if eaten
whole rather than polished or
"whitened". However, white bread
has some of the vitamins lost in
the steel milling and silk bolt-
ing, replaced.

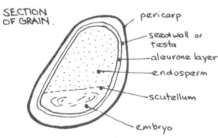

SECTION OF GRAIN.

- pericarp
- seed wall or testa
- aleurone layer
- endosperm
- scutellum
- embryo

VEGETABLES are between 90-95%
water. Of the dry matter of
leaf vegetables there is 20%
protein with a favourable mixture of amino acids, including
lysine missing from cereals.
Fresh vegetables contain vitamins
and minerals particularly
Vitamins C and A, and a carbohydrate content, the nutritional
use of which is not fully under-
stood. However, dried beans and
potatoes are storage organs rich
in readily usable carbohydrate.

FRUITS are 75-90% water, 1%
protein and certain vitamins and
minerals especially when fresh
and unpeeled. The carbohydrate
content and thus their calorific value varies greatly.

OILS & FATS Oil used to be
saved for lamps, but owing to
modern technology, the extrac-
tion of oils, mainly of vegetable origin has become common-
place. The best oils are soya,
olive, peanut, cotton seed,
sunflower seed as their high
percentage of unsaturated fatty
acid seems healthful, particularly
with regard to the cholesterol
level in the bloodstream. The
essential fatty acids necessary
for the intake of fat soluable
Vitamins A and B are found in
cereal germ, nuts, sunflower
seed oil and linseed oil.

SUGAR is another comparitively
recent addition to our diet,
owing to modern technology. It
does nothing for mass nutrition
as it contains no vitamins, protein or minerals. Only useful
as a quick source of energy in
emergencies.

SPICES have little food value
and in fact some may be toxic.
They mask the aromas of food
which are indicative of its
condition. (Useful when the
only food source does not smell
good?). However, the herbally
medicinal value of some is
probably worth consideration.

Note:
    The nutritional value of
minor food groups, fungi and
nuts is discussed in the section
on gathering.

PLANT

VEGETARIANISM

The decision to be meat eating
or vegetarian can at present only
be justified for the individual
or within the terms of a particular culture. Arguments for one
point of view can always be
countered by arguments for the
other. The best way to decide
is to experiment with yourself.
However, if you eat meat regularly in large quantities, do
not expect to be able to sudd-
enly stop eating meat and exist
happily on vegetables. The body
doesn't like sudden changes and
so you probably won't feel too
good. Dietary changes of any
type should be made gradually,
to give the body plenty of time
to adjust.

Here are some arguments for and
against being a vegetarian.

Some people see animals as beings
similar to themselves in so many
ways that they feel repulsed at
the thought of eating their
flesh. The characteristics of
plants do not have such strong
similarities and so do not
cause qualms. Countering this
point of view it is common for
people to eat an animal so that
they may be imbued with particular qualities it possesses.

Vegetarians may have to examine
the ethics of eating plants after
the recent experiments of Cleve
Backster in which he found that
plants are capable of remarkable
acts of perception and commun-
ication . His experiments, in
which he measures the minute
electrical activity of plants,
suggests that plants may "feel"
something when their destruction
is even considered in the human
mind.

Vegans are people who avoid all
animal products, including dairy
produce, because they disapprove
of the way animals are commonly
reared and treated. This seems
to imply a strong identification
with the animals' consciousness.

Ecologically based arguments for
vegetarianism contain a more
forceful logic. Pesticides used
on plants "build up" in the bodies
of animals e.g. mercury absorbed
in minute amounts by the lower
food chains of planktons may
reach dangerously poisonous concentrations by the time it reaches
the high food chains and is lod-
ged in the flesh of fish. Sec-
ondly, a given area of land will
support much more plant food
than it will live stock, so that
the growing of cereals makes more
efficient use of land than grazing. Against this often quoted
argument, is the fact that much
land that is used for grazing, is
land that it would be difficult
to make arable such as hilly up-
lands cropped by sheep.

A great deal of meat every day,
without much exercise, will certainly supply too much protein;
there is no dietetic reason why
reasonable quantities of meat
should not be consumed.

As mentioned above, meat needs
a lot more land than vegetables
and so is correspondingly more
expensive than vegetable protein. Meat doesn't keep as
well as most vegetables. This
is the reason many people are
vegetarians, it is simply cheaper
and more convenient.

One thing that meat eaters con-
tinually murmur in "vegetable
arguments" is succulence - Vegetarianism has been put down a
lot because not many people have
learned the skill necessary to
give a vegetarian meal the mouth
watering aroma to which meat
eaters are addicted.

SOYA BEANS have the four
main amino acids in similar
quantities to meat and well
within health standards.

VEGETARIAN?

YIN & YANG

are the two aims of infinity,
absolute oneness, God or the
infinite pure expansion.

YIN	============	YANG
centrefugal	....	centre petal
lightness	....	weight
cold	....	heat
dark	....	light
silence	....	sound
calm	....	action
water	....	fire
vegetable	....	animal
salad	....	cereal
female	....	male
sweet	....	salty
Vit.C	....	Vits.A,D,K

The principle food and the
foundation of macrobiotics
is cereals. Vegetables
supplement the cereals but
are used in small quantities.

Fish is used in smaller
quantities.

Animal products, fruit and oils
are used little and infrequently.

Drinks are used in the smallest
quantities possible down to 8oz.
of fluid per day.

Foods have been divided into
either Yin or Yang depending
on their relative qualities.
As a guide.
Examples of food generally
thought to be strong YIN are:-

VEGETABLES, potatoes, tomatoes,
egg plant, beans, cucumber,
asparagus, spinach, mushroom,
DAIRY PRODUCTS, butter, yoghurt,
creams.
FRUITS, pineapple, grapefruit,
bananas, figs, pears - also:
tea, coffee, fruit juices,
wine and all sugared drinks.

Foods generally thought to be
YANG are:-

CEREALS, buckwheat,
FISH roe,
VEGETABLES, carrot, burdock,
cress, dandelion root, also
egg, pheasant, goats milk,
apple.

All foods should be natural,
never artificial or industrially
prepared. Thus, whilst commercially available meat is not
considered good, wild or free
ranging birds, fresh fish and
shellfish are considered to be
OK in small amounts (compared
to the principle cereal.)

Food is eaten when in season,
unpeeled, locally grown and
chewed well.

Macrobiotics places emphasis
on care and thought.

A Western dietician might see
macrobiotics as a process of
acid Alkaline balance to create
the neutral (or slightly alkaline) body fluid.

YIN YANG principles embody an
approach to life that is not
just confined to eating. The
'objective' of Yin Yang is the
achievement of harmony and
wholeness of being

Remember: Qualities of Yin Yang
are ever changing in relation
to their changing surroundings.
Do not fall into fixed habits.

AIR

The average person eats about
2¼ lbs. of food, drinks 4½
pints of water and breathes
38lbs. of air a day. Eating
can be postponed for weeks,
water for days, but breathing
only for minutes.

There are between 150-200
different chemicals in the
exhaust fumes of petrol
engines. The exhaust fumes
from petrol engines are considerably more toxic than
diesel fumes because of the
high proportion of carbon
monoxide they contain.

In smoky towns, each ounce
of air contains millions
of pollutive particles and
Britain has the world's
highest bronchitis rate.

Lead is one of the worst
poisons in London air. It
is estimated that lead-free
petrol would reduce the lead
content of London air by one
third.

"Nourishment via odours: life
maintained by inhalation,
followed by the degeneration
of the alimentary canal."
                    John Cage.

There are 300 miles of air
over your head all the time.
You process ½ pint of air when
you inhale.

MARTINDALE PROTECTIVE MASKS

Permit Free Breathing
Clear Vision
Easy Speech

PROTECT-

your health against dust and
prevent dirt and irritants from
reaching the nose, throat and
lungs.

WARNING

Genuine MARTINDALE Refills
are safe and only they should be
used with this mask.
Substitutes can be ineffective
and dangerous.

Patentees and Sole Manufacturers:
MARTINDALE ELECTRIC CO., LTD.
Neasden Lane, London, N.W.10, England

WORKERS
ENJOY
WEARING
THEM

PLACE HEAD-
BAND WELL
UP AROUND
HEAD TO KEEP
FROM SLIPPING
DOWN

PRESS NOSE
TABS IN CLOSE
AGAINST FACE
TO HOLD PAD
AGAINST THE
NOSTRILS

PRESS EDGES
OF FACE PLATE
DOWN TO FIT
FACE SNUGLY

THE MOST POPULAR LIGHTWEIGHT MASK FOR OVER 30 YEARS!

Antarctic Survey Team use MSA
(Mine Safety Appliance Ltd.)
toxic tester to see whether

carbon monoxide is building
up to a dangerous level in
their almost completely sealed
huts.

AIR
O₂

BREATHIN1234......

O_2

BREATHE IN 1 2 3 4 5 6 7 8   BREATHE OUT 1 2 3 4.......

"TAKING a glass of water anywhere in the world, the statistical probability is that 10,000-1,000,000 water molecules in the glass were present in Julius Cæsar's urine".

Without water in 50°F air temperature you can last about 10 days. With 4 pints you can last about 11 days.
Man normally requires 3-4½ pints of water daily. Much of his water requirement will be obtained in his food.
Drink whenever thirsty .... a little and often.

"In the early stages of thirst do not use spirits, put away tobacco. A stone or leaf in the mouth prevents the tongue from swelling. If you lose between 6-10% of your body weight through water loss, dizziness and inability to walk may occur. Don't drink sea, urine, alcohol, battery water, fish fluids and anything that is milky, salty or soapy. Treat all water you are not sure of as polluted ————.

WATER

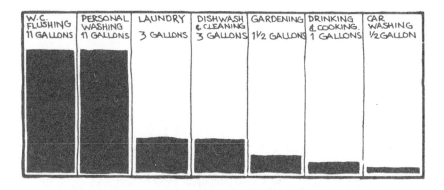

W.C. FLUSHING 11 GALLONS	PERSONAL WASHING 11 GALLONS	LAUNDRY 3 GALLONS	DISHWASH & CLEANING 3 GALLONS	GARDENING 1½ GALLONS	DRINKING & COOKING. 1 GALLONS	CAR WASHING ½ GALLON

Domestic consumption per head per day. (Figures for 1967 based on estimates by the Water Resources Board.)

CYCLE.

FINDING WATER

Streams

Check stream for at least 440 yds. upstream to ensure you are not downstream of any cattle watering areas, animal corpses, pollution outlet. Look carefully, smell, taste water. Fast flowing water is likely to be better than sluggish water. Make sure any latrines cannot drain into the stream. Drinking water should be taken highest up stream, and washing should be done downstream.

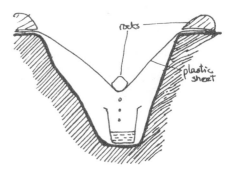

Springs

Even if the spring looks clear, have the water tested. Contamination can carry a long way underground through rock crevices or very open gravel. The flow through a half-inch pipe laid on a gradient of one foot drop to 100' in length can deliver about 500 gallons in 24 hours. So a small spring may be able to provide more water than it would at first glance seem likely.

Warning. Avoid water holes around which green plants are not thriving - it may be poisoned.

Dew. A blanket away from trees will be soaked by dew. Wring out into a basin. Bunch of grass, handkerchief or sponge brushed through dewy grass until soaked - wring out into pot.

Plants

The trunk of a beech tree has many well marked channels where the rain and condensed dew run down. The Wycombe chest makers used to make a cut across such a channel and drive in a chip of wood which diverts the water into a pail.

Quite apart from such ingenious methods, vegetables and fruits contain about 95% water. The greater part of daily water requirements may be got from food.

The Acacia tree usually has fresh water within 15 feet. Many plants will indicate water as well as soil type condition.

The Divining rod

For location of underground water on a low cost basis, nothing is so successful as a properly used divining rod. The principle is that the arm muscles are tensed by a twig or wire. When tensed, muscle seems to be affected in some way by underground water and other forces so that the diviner passes over such a source, the muscle undergoes a slight jerk which is amplified by the twig or wire. The greater the source, the stronger the affect. Guy Underwood describes the techniques in detail in his book "Patterns of the Past."

Other ways?

Some understanding of the geophysical meaning of landscape forms, will give an indication of where water is most likely to be found. There is almost certain to be a fairly reachable water

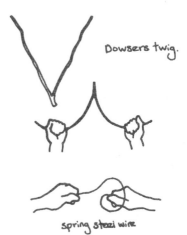

Dowsers twig.

spring steel wire

PURIFICATION

Boil questionable water at least five minutes. Nearly every unknown source in the country is "questionable". All water used in cooking, washing dishes and teeth should be so treated. To restore the air lost from boiled water and make it more palatable, the cooked water may be poured between two vessels or shaken up.

Halazone type chemical tablets will purify one pint of water per tablet used in about $\frac{1}{2}$ hour. The chemical action relies on the release of chlorine gas. Care should be taken that all parts of the container used are purified, and that drops of water, for instance, around the rim, are not left to reinfect the water later.

Chlorine in some form is regarded as the most dependable disinfectant for drinking water. Emergency chlorination of drinking water may be accomplished in three steps:
1. Dissolving one heaped teaspoon full of chloride of lime in eight quarts of water.
2. Adding one part of this solution to one hundred parts of the water to be purified.
3. Wait at least 30 minutes.

Another water purifying chemical is iodine. One drop of tincture of iodine to one quart of water, wait 30 mins. or use iodine water purification tablets containing the active Tetraglycine Hydroperiodide. Used particularly in the tropics where chlorine based tablets cannot be relied upon.

Note: wood charcoal dropped into boiling water will sweeten it and help to purify. Using this, simmer for 15-20 minutes.

A chemist will give you details of how to get a water source tested.

Vase Shape

WATER STERILISING TABLETS
Indispensable to the camper who tours abroad. Each outfit contains 50 sterilising tablets and 50 "Thio" tablets to remove brackish taste. One tablet is sufficient for 1 pint of water. Complete in handy size tin box.

Some domestic waste waters are given, primary, secondary and tertiary treatment, the product water is not only more expensive, but of higher quality (i.e. lower concentrations of significant impurities) than many waters regularly used for domestic water supply.

Purifiers are of two types, neither of which can be relied on for getting rid of small virus.

The Pasteur-Chamberlain porous porcelain pot type Domestic installations are capable of dealing with 3-16 gallons or more per day.

The silicated Carbon/charcoal purifiers are made in many sizes ranging from the portable model shown below to domestic units. Carbon cartridge has to be replaced at regular intervals.

AQUAPAC   Portable Water Purifier
The perfect pocket-sized miniature portable drinking water purifier. An adequate supply of safe, delicious, contaminant-free water is available from any non-salt water source for a whole family for as long as a month with a simple disposable cartridge. May be operated by gravity or with easy-to-use hand pump.
Dimensions: $5\frac{1}{2}''$ Diameter, $1\frac{1}{2}''$ Wide.
Carrying weight: 9 ounces.

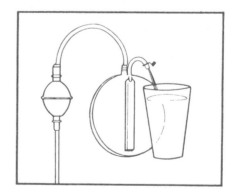

New Excursion Collapsible Filter will fit on any ordinary Tumbler or Water Bottle, and yields a glass of pure and perfectly wholesome water.

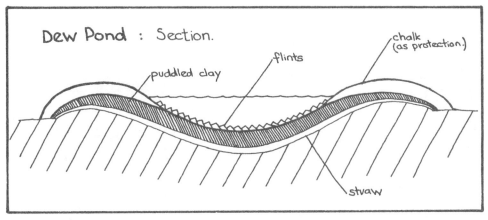

Dew Pond : Section.

puddled clay
flints
chalk (as protection.)
straw

ROOF COLLECTION

Where there is no ground water or it is badly polluted a good arrangement is to collect rain water from the roof via the normal gutter and drain pipe, and store it in an underground tank.

The storage tank is often built underground to avoid the water being warmed or frozen.

The amount of rain water which can be collected in tanks of this sort depends on average annual rainfall and the available collecting area. Theoretically, 1" of rainfall over 100sq.ft. will give about 50 gallons allowing for evaporation losses.

In this country, the rainfall from an average house roof will probably have to be supplemented by collecting from a barn roof or similar to provide the average total water needs. Despite its advantages this system is not widely used, although it may be much cheaper than digging a well to construct the necessary storage tank.

The straw cuts off the heat of the earth and when moist mists flow over the cooler pond, they condense on its surface. This could have been the method used by prehistoric man who inhabited the many hill forts around the country.

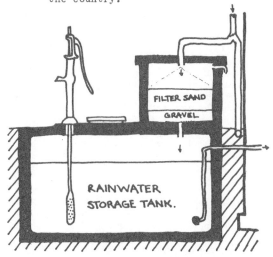

FILTER SAND
GRAVEL

RAINWATER STORAGE TANK.

Solarstill one method of obtaining water from seawater or dirty water is by distillation using the warmth of the sun, trapped under glass, to evaporate the water. It is easy to make yourself. About ½pint of water per day per square foot of glass is obtained in the winter, going up to going up to 7 pints in the summer.

GOVERNMENT SURPLUS
SOLAR STILL
LIMITED QUANTITY ONLY
For the production of drinking water.
Must have cost thousands to perfect.
£3 each
CARRIAGE PAID
DRINKING WATER

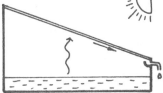

WELL well WELL

There are three principal methods of well construction, all of them useful in particular conditions.

1. Hand-dug Wells are still one of the cheapest methods of providing water for a village, but it is relatively expensive for the family or small group. This type of well is capable of providing up to a few hundred gallons per hour.

The first consideration is the diameter. The narrower the well the cheaper is the lining. However, the smallest diameter within which one man can work is about $3\frac{1}{4}'$, and for two men you need $4\frac{1}{4}'$.

A lining of permanent materials is always necessary to prevent collapse and stop polluted water from entering. It also serves as a foundation for the well top. It is best that the lining is built in place as the construction proceeds from both a safety and economic point of view.
An alternative to actually building in situ is the caissoning method in which a prefabricated lining is sunk. The best lining material is concrete between 3/5" thick and reinforced. Metal shuttering is usually used and between 3ft and 15ft are dug at a time depending on the structure of the soil.

When the underground water is reached, the well may be dug deeper by the caissioning method of bailing out water as work progresses. Water may enter the well either by porous walls of the caissioned section or through an open bottom. Porous walls are more usual, allowing the bottom to be concreted up to facilitate cleaning and prevent upward movement of soil.

Tube Wells
Driven These are constructed by ramming a 3" pipe into the ground. The lower end of the pipe is fitted with a drive-well point, the porous side of which allows the water to enter the pipe. These wells may be driven through compact soils and even chalk, but they cannot be driven into rocky strata or heavy clay.

pozzo (pot'sō), n.; pl. pozzi (-sē). [It., a well < L. puteus, a well: see pit[1].] In Venice, on

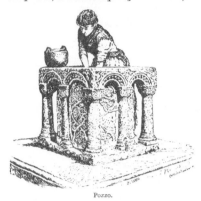

Pozzo.

of the curbs or heads of the cisterns which are filled with water from the neighboring mainland; a well-curb: a common abbreviation of vera di pozzo.

When the water bearing stratum is reached, and the pipe end is well into it, the drive well point is cleared by over pumping to remove fine particles around the head. If water is not found, or the ground is deemed unsuitable, the pipe may be levered out and measured to a new site. This is one of the great advantages of the driver well. Its disadvantage over the hand dug well is the greater amount of equipment necessary.

Jetted With a small amount of pumping equipment, wells of up to 300' can be sunk quickly. Disadvantage: plenty of water needs to be available; however, it may be re-cycled. Water is driven into a tube that is twisted and driven into the ground. The water flows up the outside of the pipe, carrying large amounts of soil in a light mud suspension. The pipes are sunk in 20 foot lengths. The jetted water is re-used, by allowing the dirt and sand to settle out in a reservoir sump.

Bored A simple method of constructing a small diameter shallow well is with an earth borer - operated by hand. Suitable for soft soil, chalk limestone and alluvial formulas, which are devoid of large gravel and stones and can be easily penetrated. Larger drilling rigs are of very high capital cost and need specialist firms.

If a pump is fitted, overpumping must be avoided as this may induce caving in.

WELLS

PUMPS

Pumping problems are often the reason for the breakdown of small water supply systems. The most common pump types for small water-supply systems are:

1. Centrifugal pumps above ground, power operated.

2. Reciprocating pumps above ground, hand or power operated.

3. Reciprocating pumps with the cylinder in the well. Deep wells may be operated by hand, power or wind.

4. Turbine pumps for deep wells, driven from the surface or from a submersible electric motor.

5. Jet pumps, above ground, power driven.

6. Hydraulic rams.

7. Continuous belt or bucket pumps.

8. Archimedian screw pumps.

The pressure of air at sea level will hold a column of water in a pipe 34 ft. high, if there is a perfect vacuum above it. In practice the distance of the pump cylinder to the water surface cannot be more than about 20ft. due to the inevitable mechanical inefficiency of pumps. The reciprocating pump is most widely used. It is able to be used by a variety of people, animals and other power sources. It will last a long time, as its mode of action is slow, it is easy to maintain, it is robust with few parts to break or go wrong & low cost.
With water deeper than 16 ft. underground, the cylinder is attached to a drop-pipe and placed underground within 16 ft. of the water table. The depth will determine how much water can be pumped with a given time/effect. For a 20ft. lift, one man may pump 9 gallons per minute, for a 100ft. lift, he can pump only $1\frac{1}{2}$ gallons.

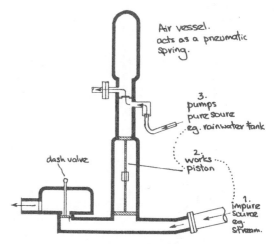

Air vessel. acts as a pneumatic spring.

3. pumps pure source eg. rainwater tank

2. works piston

1. impure source eg. stream.

dash valve

This pump will use the pressure of water from an impure water source such as a polluted stream to raise water from a pure source such as a well. A ram will work with an 18" head but 3ft. is best. One seventh of the water entering a simple ram can be raised to four times the height of the head.

The considerations for choosing a pump.
1. Maintenance service available.

2. Capital cost of pump and equipment.

3. Operating cost.

4. Capacity and lift required.

When a large amount of water is required for irrigation or to supply a large community, wind pumps are the best, low cost power source.

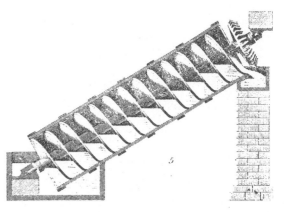

Screw of Archimedes

PUMPS

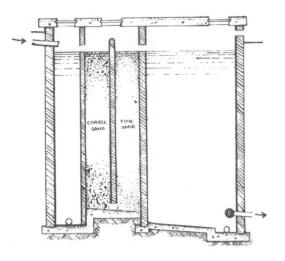

COARSE SAND   FINE SAND

If the tank or cistern form the sole domestic water supply, it should have a working capacity of not less than 1,500 gallons.

The tank must be completely impervious, especially if below ground to stop pollutive source entering.

If a water storage tank is situated at a point relatively high compared with a drainaway point at which a small turbine may be installed, the water acts as an energy storage, so that, for instance, water may be pumped into the tank with a wind powered pump during windy periods.

In calm periods, the water is allowed to fall through the turbine which may generate electricity, heat or do other work (e.g. milling.)

P.S. A method of small volume storage for camp sites etc., are the plastic containers that wine and cider are kept in. Off licences usually give these away free, and if you make a carrier for them, they are ideal, holding 5 gallons and having taps fitted.
If water is stored in porous pots or canvas, it will keep cool.

COLLAPSIBLE WATER BOTTLE
Capacity 1 gallon
Complete with handle. Folds flat.

DAM

No attempt to make a dam holding 15ft. or more head of water, should be made without engineering advice. This should be obtained, if at all possible, even with smaller projects.

Having chosen a site, and made sure that there will be enough water that sufficient reservoir capacity may be obtained, and that the foundations are firm, it is necessary to choose suitable material for its construction, The material used should be uniform clay sand soil (no boulders!). The material must be spread on continuous shallow layers 4-6" deep over the whole area; it must be damp, but not too wet; each layer must be well compacted.

Note: Water must never under any circumstances flow over the top of an earthen dam, a good spillway is essential.

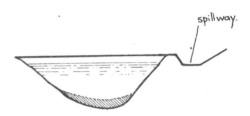

spillway.

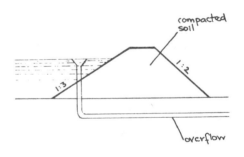

compacted soil

1:2

1:3

overflow

Semba-koki

3. *Finishing Steam Thrashing Machine.*

GROWTH

Anyone can grow plants; in fact they grow on their own needing only care and attention to bring them to fruition. With skill developed through experience over a long time you will be able to get massive crops individually huge in size, succulent and beautiful to behold; but anyone who wants to can just grow some plants.

A ten rod plot measuring roughly 30ft x 90ft (ie. less than 1/16 of an acre) can be made capable of supplying vegetables for a family of four or five. This is roughly as big a plot as the average man can handle in his spare time.

❋ A 240ft row of potatoes gives about 4 cwt.

❋ A 60ft x 90ft plot will produce sufficient wheat to supply one man with bread for a year. This includes enough flour for cake, pastries et al.

❋ Under glass plants will grow quicker, earlier in the year and more thickly. The most simple cloche will achieve results; cold-frames take up very little room; and the greenhouse, whilst being relatively inexpensive will enable growing in 3 dimensions and also provide a fragrant, if humid, spare room.

❋ Leeks crop all through the winter and at 5 P. a packet will give you anything up to 200 plants. Cabbage is a similar crop that grows throughout the winter and is very versatile in the kitchen cooked or raw.

❋ There are literally hundreds of methods of preparing something as humble as the potato to be found in common cook-books. If you are going to live on simple home-grown food and hand-gathered herbs it is necessary to learn some of the old peasant culinary expertise.

❋ "Digging a new garden is to some a dreary task but to others it is a joyful days exercise. Nothing is more exhilarating in cold winter weather; but it must be done properly with a sharp shining spade, a steady rythmn and ten minutes break every hour to enjoy the sight and smell of the newly turned earth."
Amateur Gardening Magazine.

CROP ROTATION gives plant

diseases time to die out and makes good use of manure leading to a balanced soil. Similar species (ie weakness to similar pests.) will not follow each other. This is a 3 year scheme.

B	A	C
C	B	A
A	C	B
1	2	3

CABBAGE	
SAVOYS · intercrop with early carrots.	
BRUSSEL SPROUTS · early beet.	**B**
SPROUTING BROCCOLI	
KALE	
SWEDES	
GLOBE BEET	
EARLY DWARF PEAS	
DWARF PEAS intercrop with spinach or lettuce	
DWARF PEAS	
ONIONS follow with Spring Cabbage.	**C**
SHALLOTS follow with Winter Lettuce.	
BROAD BEANS intercrop with summer lettuce.	
RUNNER BEANS	
PARSNIPS	
CARROTS	**A**
POTATOES (early) follow with Turnips or Toms.	
POTATOES	
BEET or SWEDES.	

GROWING SCRAPS

Photo courtesy of Museum of English Rural Life, Reading, BERKSHIRE.

Vegetable Planting Chart

	VEGFTABLE	Rows apart feet	Plants apart in row, inches	Planting depth, inches	Seed for 50 feet	Days to germin-ation	Days to yield	Buy plants or seeds	Possible yield per 50 feet of row	For a family of five, Summer and Winter Supplies: Row Length	No. of Plantings	Common Insect Pests and Suggested Control
Very hardy. Not injured by winter freezing.	**Artichoke, Jerusalem**	3	20	3	½ peck	8–12	120–140	P	1½ bu.	100	1	Seldom bothered.
	Asparagus	2½	20	6	30 plants	8–10	2 yrs.	P	25 bunches of 1 dz. each	100	....	Asparagus beetle. Rotenone.
	Parsnip	1½	4	½	1 pkt.	15–20	80–100	S	150 roots	50	1	Seldom bothered.
	Rhubarb	4	48	¼	10 plants	......	2–3 Yrs.	P	180 stalks	50	....	Seldom bothered.
Hardy. Withstand light frost but not freezing. Plant when ground is easily prepared.	**Beet**	1½–2	3–4	½	½ oz.	7–10	60– 75	S	150 roots	100	3	Seldom bothered.
	Chard, Swiss	2	15	½	½ oz.	7–10	50 & on	S	15 plants	20	1	Blister beetle. Rotenone or hand pick.
	Broccoli	2	18	¼	1 pkt.	6– 9	70– 80	P	30 heads	50	1	Same as cabbage.
	Brussels Sprouts	2	18	¼	1 pkg.	6– 9	70 & on	P	30 qts.	30	1	Same as cabbage.
	Cabbage, early	2	12	¼	1 pkt.	6– 9	65– 75	P	50 heads	50	1	Green Cabbage Worm. Rotenone.
	Cabbage, late	2	18	¼	1 pkt.	6– 9	80–100	P	35 heads	50	1	Aphis. Nicotine dust or spray.
	Chinese Cabbage	2	12	¼	1 pkt.	6– 9	75– 85	S	50 heads	50	2	Same as cabbage.
	Carrot	1½	3	¼	1 pkt.	12–18	60– 75	S	200 roots	100	3	Seldom bothered.
	Cauliflower	2	18	¼	1 pkt.	5–10	55– 65	P	35 heads	50	2	Same as cabbage.
	Celeriac	2	4	⅛	1 pkt.	15–20	90–120	S	150 bulbs	25	2	Same as celery.
	Celery	2–3	5	⅛	1 pkt.	15–20	120–150	S	120 plants	50	2	Aphis. Nicotine dust or spray, Celery Leaf Tyer-Pyrethrum.
	Chicory, Witloof	2	10	¼	1 pkt.	8–12	for winter	S	60 roots	50	1	Green Caterpillar. Pyrethrum or hand pick.
	Collard	2½	24	¼	1 pkt.	6– 9	90 & on	S	25 plants	50	2	Same as cabbage.
	Endive	1½	9	¼	1 pkt.	10–14	70– 80	S	60 plants	30	1	Seldom bothered.
	Kale	2½	24	¼	1 pkt.	6– 9	70– 80	S	25 plants	25	1	Same as cabbage.
	Kohlrabi	2	8	¼	1 pkt.	6– 9	55– 65	S	70 bulbs	50	2	Same as cabbage.
	Leek	1½	6	½	1 pkt.	7–10	120–150	S	100 stems	30	1	Onion Thrip. Nicotine sulphate and soap solution or tartar emetic.
	Lettuce, leaf	2	12	¼	1 pkt.	6– 8	45– 50	S	50 heads	50	1	Cut Worm. Poison bait on ground. Aphis. Nicotine dust or spray.
	Lettuce, head	2	12	¼	1 pkt.	6– 8	50– 70	P	50 heads	50	1	Birds. Cover with screen or open-meshed cloth.
	Mustard	2	9	¼	1 pkt.	5– 8	60– 75	S	50 plants	20	2	Same as cabbage.
	Onion	1½	3–4	½	1 pkt. or 1 pint sets	7–10	90–110	S or P	150–200 bulbs	50	1	Onion Thrip. Nicotine sulphate and soap solution or tartar emetic.
	Parsley	1½	4	¼	1 pkt.	15–20	85–100	S	150 bunches	30	1	Seldom bothered.
	Peas	2–3	1–2	1	½ lb.	7–10	60– 80	S	25–50 quarts	100	3	Aphis. Rotenone, pyrethrum, or nicotine dust or spray.
	Potato, white	3	12	4	3 lbs.	8–12	80–120	P	60–80 lbs.	100	2	Same as tomato.
	Radish	1	1–2	½	1 pkt.	3– 6	25– 60	S	300–600	25	4	Cabbage Maggot. Avoid by quick root growth.
	Spinach	1½	6	¾	1 pkt.	7–12	40– 50	S	100 plants	50	2	Aphis. Nicotine dust or spray.
	Turnip	1½	4–6	¼	1 pkt.	5–10	50– 80	S	100–150 roots	50	2	Aphis. Nicotine dust or spray.
	Turnip, Rutabaga	2	6	¼	1 pkt.	5–10	80– 90	S	100 roots	50	1	Seldom bothered.
Tender. Easily injured by frost. Don't plant until all danger of late frost is over.	**Beans, bush**	2–2½	3–4	1½	4 oz.	5– 8	50– 70	S	20 qts.	100	4	Mexican Bean Beetle. Rotenone.
	Beans, pole	3–4	9, or hills	1½	4 oz.	5– 8	65– 80	S	30 qts.	50	1	pyrethrum, or cryolite. Flea beetle, red spiders
	Corn, early	2½	9	1	1 oz.	5– 8	70– 80	S	50 ears	80	1	Corn borer. Apply rotenone dust just before ear forms, then 4 times more 5 days apart.
	Corn, main crop	3	12	1	1 oz.	5– 8	80– 95	S	50 ears	100	1	Corn Ear Worm. Snip off tips of ears after silk dries or apply mineral oil to ear tips.
	Cucumber	4	24	¾	1 pkt.	7–10	60– 70	S	150–200 pickles	50	1	Striped Cucumber Beetle. Rotenone. Aphis. Nicotine dust or spray.
	Pumpkin	8	60	1	¼ oz.	7–12	110–130	S	25–30 fruits	25	1	Squash Bug. Rotenone or hand pick. Other Pests. Same as cucumber.
	Squash, bush	4	36	1	1 pkt.	7–10	55– 65	S	75–100 fruits	50	1	Same as pumpkin.
	Squash, vining	6	60	1	1 pkt.	7–10	65–120	S	40– 80 fruits	25	1	Cut Worm. Paper collar around each plant when set out.
	Tomato	3–4	36	½	1 pkt.	7–12	75– 90	P	175–200 lbs.	75	2	Green Tomato Worm. Dust with rotenone or hand pick. Aphis. Nicotine dust or spray.

CHART

SUFFICIENT

Self subsistence farming is producing your food requirements in your 'spare time'. The innate desire to grow things and be self sufficient is within most men.

The maximum amounts of food required for a family of four + occasional friends are about, 400 gallons of milk, 2400 eggs, 60 poultry, 52 rabbits, 200 lbs of honey, 200 lbs of butter and 3000—4000 lbs of vegetables for one year. The amount of land necessary to be self suffi-cient varies between 1—7 acres depending on the quality of the land and your diet. Less than one acre of good land is needed for vegetables whereas three acres are necessary for two cows. A wooded acre, an orchard and a 'wilderness' make up the 'ideal' 7 acre holding. Choose your land carefully. It should have a southern aspect with good soil. Dig trial holes for yourself. Especially avoid sand and gravel or land that is boggy in the winter (although a small pond is useful.) Land should be bought with some dwelling, even if derelict, on it. The hassles of staying on land without officially accepted buildings on it are likely to be great.

Fencing is a important consideration. You'll find a carefully cultivated speciality trampled by neighbouring animals or eaten by rabbits if the land is not well fenced.

When you have got your holding buy the largest scale ordinance survey map of the district and plan the layout of your holding.

Soft Fruits: plant these as soon as you have decided on their position. Be advised on the best varieties for the district by the county horticultural expert.

Vegetables: to extend the growing season simple cloche cultivation has many advantages; another method is to protect part of the garden with a simple earth parapet to east, west and north. It is well worth aiming to grow a surplus in varieties that can suppliment livestock winter rations.

Poultry: up to an acre can be given to poultry. One must decide on the amount of table-birds and pure egg producers when choosing breeds. It is also not to be forgotten that poultry can be decorative as well as purely functional.

Rabbits: breed quickly and are easy to keep. Ideal meat-stock for the self-subsister. However plenty of wild rabbits, that need to be kept down, may be available.

Milk: the question of cows or goats. Advantage of the cow is that it may be left out in all weathers, whereas goats need more attention but less space. note: different common livestock are discussed in the section on Rearing.

Housing Stock: wherever possible use concrete floors and interconnect buildings with dry walks. In building outhouses ingenuity and inventiveness are valuable qualities, and it is normally possible to erect most of the shelter necessary using materials to be found around and about the locality.

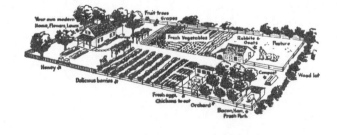

Your own modern Home, Flowers, Lawns · Fruit trees Grapes · Fresh Vegetables · Rabbits & Goats · Pasture · Honey · Delicious berries · Fresh eggs Chickens to eat · Orchard · Compost · Wood lot · Bacon Ham, Fresh Pork

ORGANIC

Organic farming aims to reduce the need for harmful or unnecess--ary inorganic content in soil such as artificial pesticides or fertilisers, by producing a naturally fertilised and balanced soil ecosystem.
Compost making and pest control without poisons are the critical skills involved.

'Composting' is widely known as a big heap of multiferous waste that naturally rots away over the course of a year to form 'manure'. There are however specific methods of building, managing and adding to this heap which will bring it to fruition faster and produce a more fertile compost.

The Composting heap must be shaded from sun and wind, on the north side of a wall or shed. A trench is then dug about 6ft. wide and 6-12 inches deep. The depth should not penetrate the topsoil; if it does, the bottom of this shallow pit should be relined with topsoil. The length of the trench might be 10ft for a small garden up to 100ft or more for a smallholding. Vegetable wastes are then tipped into the trench. Materials that may be used include; household food scraps, toppings, leftovers, couch grass (esp. valuable) roadside weeds, spoiled hay, soft potatoes, slaughterhouse wastes, brushwood, twigs, ditch and pond scrappings, lawn cuttings, hedge clippings, leaves............and so on.
The greater the diversity the better the compost is likely to be; especially if you include wild herbs such as nettles, yarrow, chamomile, dandelion, oakbark.

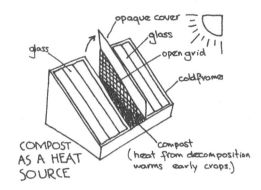

COMPOST AS A HEAT SOURCE

opaque cover
glass
open grid
cold frame
glass
compost (heat from decomposition warms early crops.)

Spread each layer evenly and not too thickly in the trench. Each layer is then sprinkled lightly with slaked lime. To each 6-12 inches of waste add a layer of soil, perhaps the same which earlier was dug out to make the trench, and work it in well with a fork. The heap is built up in this way until it is 4 or 5 feet high.

The heap must be well aerated so make sure that if you are using vegetation likely to compact you alternate layers of twigs and broken up brushwood or construct vents with bundles of scrubwood as shown in the diagram. If the heap becomes dry sprinkle water onto it. When the heap is finished it is covered with soil or sodden straw; and may be protected with a sheet of plastic in very damp districts.

A gully is then made along the top of the heap and the essential animal nitrogenous compound added in the form of urine. Use liquid stable manure if you are not able to make regular visits to the heap yourself or it is to large for you to manage. An alternative method of obtaining these nitrogenous compounds is by mixing fresh manure or bonemeal within the layers.
The heap is then left over the winter. In Spring the heap is turned inside out; the top layers being put at the bottom, the bottom layers at the top. The mixture is loosened up to improve aeration. This turnover is best done working progressively from one end having previously left an extra 6 foot of trench to make this possible.
The compost will be ready in the autumn or following spring.

The basis of many 'organic' soil rehabilitation methods is the BIO--DYNAMIC theory initiated by Rudolf Steiner in the 1920s; however some of the strange detailed actions he proposed have given the organic movement an eccentric air. Details from Secretary Rudolf Steiner House, 35 Park Rd. London NW1.

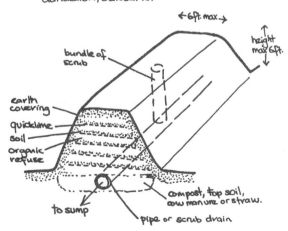

←6ft. max→
height max 6ft.
bundle of scrub
earth covering
quicklime
soil
organic refuse
compost, top soil, cow manure or straw.
to sump
pipe or scrub drain

COMPOST

NO POISONS !

A pest is an organism that has become too numerous for mans' comfort. Usually too small and numerous to be fought by hand, a prevalent technique is to use poisonous chemicals — pesticides. However there are two points of immediate global importance concerning the rash use of poisons;

    1. When 'the pest' is present in smaller numbers it will nearly always play some ecologically significant role. In such case it would be bad to wipe out the creature.

    2. The chemicals used might derange organisms, other than the pest at which it is aimed, for some considerable period after the 'pest danger' has finished.

The aim of Biological Pest Control is to either use degradable pesticides or to increase the numbers of some other organism whose natural prey is the pest. eg. the cat kept to catch mice. Many common wild organisms are good general garden pest controllers examples being the Ladybird and the Hedgehog.

Chemical cultivation of vast tracts of land with single crops is a practice that has been condemned because of the increased danger of soil erosion; but another danger is that the removal of hedgerows and sterilising of the soil, which is encouraged by government grants, will destroy the essential communities of plants, birds and insects that live in them.

Up to now we have dumped about one billion pounds of D.D.T. into our environment. we are adding some 100,000,000 pounds each year. The effects of D.D.T. can take 30 years to become apparent. D.D.T. poisoning is <u>now</u> evident in several organisms. For example the seals who are turning on their young and killing them........ ....so even if we stop using D.D.T. today...............?

Degradable pesticides: 'Derris' and 'pyrethum' are safe general pesticides 'Quassia' is even safer than the above two and will not harm Ladybirds or bees. The cheapest strong biodegradable pesticide is nicotine; made by boiling 4 oz of tobacco dog ends in a gallon of water for ½ hour; or your could grow your own with the attendant danger of poisoning yourself in the presence of abundant smokes.

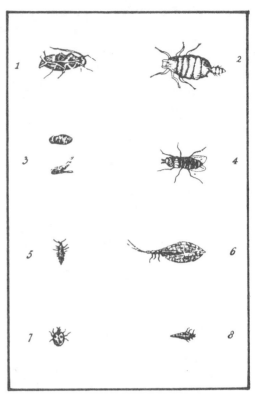

Plate IX

"The most ingenious manner of destroying the aphis would be effected by the propagation of its greatest enemy, the larva of the aphidivorous fly; of which I have given a print, and which is said by Reaumeur [Reamur], Tom. III Mem.9, to deposit its eggs, where the aphis abounds; and that, as soon as the larvae are produced, they devour hundreds around them with the necessity of no other movements but by turning to the right or left, arresting the aphis as sucking its juices. If these eggs could' be collected and carefully preserved during the winter, and properly disposed on nectarine and peach trees in the early spring, or protected from injury in hot-houses; it is probable, that this plague of the aphis might be counteracted by the natural means of devouring one insect by another; as the serpent of Moses devoured those of the magicians"

    from 'Phytologia' by Erasmus Darwin. 1800.

Plate IX above is a reproduction from "Phytologia" and shows aphids in the top row, and insects predatory on them below. 2."an aphis from which a young one is suspended for sometime after it is otherwise born". 8. is the larva of a ladybird. The lower image of 3. is the larva of the fly, shown in 4., with an aphis in its mouth.

for more details see: 'Pest Control without Poisons' available from Henry Doubleday Association, Bocking, Braintree, Essex.

PEST CONTROL

CELLAR SUCCULENTS

Many unwanted places, such as under the stairs may be made productive by growing mushrooms. 50°F is an ideal temperature. There is little watering to do and if you use modern substrate mixtures no smell or mess.

Fish-box growing trays are available direct from the manufacturers. They give 5-6 sq. ft. growing area. The compost used may be horse, pig or poultry manure, or artificially activated fertiliser

Mushrooms are an ideal complement to poultry. 20 hens and 200 sq ft. of mushrooms can be accomodated within a very small area. Used mushroom compost may be used in the vegetable garden or in potting; no waste.

You can expect a one lb. crop for each square foot; when you become more experienced you may expect to achieve 2-4 lbs. sq. ft.

Bedsit method: Collect horse manure in plastic bags. Sprinkle mushroom spawn on the broken up manure within the bag. Store at 50°F and tie up the top of the sack. This enclosed atmosphere cultivation is known as mulching and the bags should need little or no attention until the crop is ready.

Outside growing: crop being dependant on the weather. Crop is generally prolific following a dry summer. To plant a meadow or lawn you must lift the turf and place a layer of compost or manure onto the soil. Spawn is then inserted and the turf is replaced removing a little soil so that it regains ground level.

These plantings can be made at intervals of about 6 ft. Common salt or superphosphate added in late July will increase the cropping. The mushrooms will take about 3 weeks to mature from the appearance of the first pin heads. This outdoor method procures the finest mush--rooms but is unreliable.

If boxes are to be stacked outside stack them against a wall and make sure they are protected from the wind with plastic sheet or sacking to maintain the necessary humidity.

Why is it always the one variety that is grown. Many other species of mushroom are larger and more tasty and could be successfully cultivated. Eighty years ago Mr. Burbidge Curator of Trinity College Botanic Gardens, Dublin urged the cultivation of Parasol Agaric as a better food than the commonly grown Agaricus campestris. He also named Chantarelle, the Fistulina and some Boleti as well worth trying.

Anyone can grow mushrooms any--where; attics, sheds, mines, under beds, under stairs, verandas, terraces, caves, stables, derelicts, empty office blocks, block houses, under bridges, roof tops, cellars, courtyards et al.

GOODBYE NATURE?

Growing food without natural soil allows a high degree of control and intensity of production. A great deal of good quality plant food may be grown within a small space. Hydroponic culture replaces the soil or compost with a completely inert material such as sand, gravel, vermiculite or ash to act as a medium of support for the plant structure. Carefully balanced chemical solutions supply all the plants mineral nutritive requirements. Even the sunlight may be replaced with artificial lighting and of course the temperature and humidity may be exactly controlled.

Nutrient Solution : the use of chemical nutrients might be thought of as costly, but in fact, it is more economical than adding fertilisers to soil. The nutrient chemicals consist of the normal cheap commercial fertilisers. It is essential to use correctly balanced nutrient solutions to obtain results as good or better than normal natural soil production.

Any clean nonpoisonous water supply may be used. However the pH or acidity value of the water to be used must be discovered by analysis. The ideal pH value for plants is between pH 5 and pH 7 or slightly acid (pH 7 being neutral.) Most chemists will be able to supply the indicator papers necessary for a pH test. If the water is below pH 5 ie. too acid, then the alkalinity must be raised by the addition of sodium of potassium hydroxide (caustic soda and caustic potash.) To correct a water which is too alkaline (ie. above pH 7.) then add small amounts of sulphuric acid.

Elements necessary :————

Nitrogen	200	parts per million.
Potassium	200	p.p.m.
Phosphorus	65	p.p.m.
Magnesium	50	p.p.m.
Calcium	250	p.p.m.
Iron	5	p.p.m.
Boron	1	p.p.m.
Manganese	1	p.p.m.
Copper	½	p.p.m.
Zinc	½	p.p.m.

solution may be recirculated several times.

For 50 gallons of water the following compounds supply the necessary major elements in an economical mix. Dissolve in the order given.

Magnesium Sulphate	4.25 ounces
Super phosphate (16%)	7.5 ounces
Potassium Sulphate	4.0 ounces
Ammonium Sulphate	2.0 ounces
Sodium Nitrate	7.75 ounces

Note: the proportion of ammonium sulphate to sodium nitrate could be increased, particularly in the summer, to reduce the sodium content.

Trace elements for 800 gallons (keep as stock solution) mix in order as below.

Boric acid	0.72 ounces
Zinc sulphate	0.28 ounces
Manganese sulphate	0.52 ounces
Copper Sulphate	0.25 ounces

These are mixed in 4 pints of water to make the stock solution and 5 fluid ounces is added to each 50 gallons of the solution of major elements.
2.8 ounces of ferric ammonium citrate dissolved in 2 pints of water is kept separately to supply the necessary iron. 5 fluid ounces is added to each 50 gallons as above.

If you want to experiment first with small amounts of solution you can buy the trace elements ready mixed dry. Then to make up 10 gallons of nutrient you need :—

magnesium sulphate	0.9 ounces
potassium sulphate	0.5 ounces
potassium nitrate	0.5 ounces
calcium nitrate	2.0 ounces

Your water supply may contain sufficient of the trace elements already. Experiment by leaving elements out.

TO subsist successfully from gathering a dual approach seems best. First get to know well the poisonous varieties from a reliable book on the subject, then guided by oral advice, arcane knowledge, a variety of second hand herb books or a botanical identification 'flora' such as Keble Martin, identify and test plants that are recognisable and thus slowly get to know the hedgerow. But here a warning - many a hedgerow and other wilderness are today sprayed with toxic substances. It is as well to make enquiries in the area to see if this is likely.

Herbs that grow in the fields are better than those that growe in gardens, and those that growe in the hills be best.   15C herbalist.

FUNGI AS FOOD

Some fungi are very poisonous so identification must be made with care.

Fungi have been recorded as a staple food in ancient times ——— although the digestive tracts of such people may have adapted to deal more fully with them than we can.

Food Value: generally speaking mushrooms have a carbohydrate content of about 4% and a calorific value of 200-300 calories per kg. which is similar to the cabbage. ie. fairly low but useful. The protein content is also about 4% which is 1/6 that of beef but several times higher than most vegetables.
Vitamins A, B and D are present as are most of the essential mineral salts, also folic acid and an enzyme that aids digestion.

Risk of Poisoning?
1. The distinguishing features of the poisonous fungi are reasonably easy to learn.
2. There are about ten common edible species which have very distinctive features and colours.
3. Beginners should disregard all other species, especially small ones.
4. Consult a good wild mushroom book and if possible take the advice of someone with experience, at least when beginning.

※ The usual treatment for poisoning is to administer an emetic such as tepid mustard and water; and, when that has acted, to give milk. Send for a doctor at once and be careful to keep all vomited matter and the remains of any food that has been eaten for him to see.

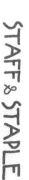

STAFF & STAPLE

Common Mushroom (*Agaricus campestris*).

ACORN & BEECHMAST

The seed crops of both Oak and Beech vary from year to year, the heaviest crops (which provide a great deal of food.) are yielded by trees over 60 years old. The species of oak that produce the best edible mast are said to be Holme oak and other ever-green varieties such as Q.ballota. It was these that formed the staple food of certain mediteronean people in antiquity. Another rule of thumb is that the biggest are the sweetest, however they should be brown and well ripe.

The degree of bitterness in acorns and beechmast is caused by the amount of tannin. This substance is poisonous in large amounts but as it is water soluble it is easily removed. Easiest method is to shell'em, grind'em, drop'em into boiling water, wait until it goes dark, pour off water. Repeat this last action several times then leave in running water or a stream for up to 12 hours.

Food Value	Acorns	Beech
Protein %	5·2	20
Fat %	43	55
Carbohydrate%	45	15
Water %	6·3	8

The dried crushed fruit may be ground into a meal and used to bake with. Acorn bread is possible; or the whole meats may be extra leached in boiling brine for 15 minutes then deep fried. They can also pickled. Beechnuts are said to be best baked and salted.
Another common nut of more popular usage is the sweet chesnut whose fruit does not need leaching.

"Heroes of Earth,
When fed with oaken mast,
The aged trees themselves,
in years surpassed."
Abraham Cowley 1614-67

ACORN. Where found: common, widespread. Part used: all. Time
gathered: bark & rinds - May, leaves - fresh or dried, acorns -
October. Preparation: ground as a flour substitute, roasted as a
coffee substitute (husks esp.), Medicinal: oak rinds in milk as
an antidote to many vegetable poisons. 5% protein, 20% fat, 60%
carbohydrate.

ALFALFA - Medicago sativa. Where found: from S.E. Europe, cultivated, locally naturalised. Part used: Young tender leaves, flow-
ering tops. Time gathered: Spring to early Summer. Preparation:
Eat uncooked. Add to vegetable salad, or prepared as a cereal
(ground alfalfa leaves as a cereal substitute), dried as a tisane.
Medicinal: excellent source of quickly assimilated vitamin and
minerals, important blood food - e.g. cure of jaundice.

ALMOND nut. Where found: as a stray from cultivation. Part used:
nut fruit. Time gathered: September/October. Preparation: used
as a substitute for animal protein. Culpepper "it rejoiceth the
heart and comforteth the brain."

ANGELICA wild. Where found: common by streamsides. Part used:
leaves, stems, roots and seeds. Time gathered: leaves - Spring,
stems - Summer, seeds before ripening, roots of first years
growth, September. Preparation: roots should be dried first -
conserve. Addition to soups and stews. Roots may be candied.
Stems may be blanched and served as asparagus.

ARROWROOT. Part used: corns - care must be taken in digging as
they are straggling. Preparation: dried, eaten as a potato substitute (baked or boiled). Ground to flour for biscuits, puddings
etc.

ASH. Part used: seeds. Time gathered: August. Preparation:
young tender ashen key fruits make a good pickle.

BARBERRY. Where found: dry woods, garden hedge. Part used: scarlet fruits. Time gathered: Autumn (Sept/Oct). Preparation: as
they are very "sharp", best to make jams and jelly, also make a
good drink. Medicinal: relieves fevered thirst and kidney colic.

BARKS - birch, lodgepole, pine, poplar, slippery elm. Part used:
inner barks. Possible south east side best. Preparation: powdered may be used as flour. Medicinal: slippery elm is a
digestant.

BEDSTRAW, GOOSE GRASS, CLEAVERS - Galium aparine. Where found:
most thickets, common. Part used: early sprouts, seeds. Time
gathered: Spring to early Summer. Preparation: steamed or salad
(seeds offer a good substitute for coffee). Medicinal: A "reducing" herb. See Gerard. An infusion of the dried plant clivers
is said to be a cure for colds.

BEECHNUT nut. Where found: common, widespread. Part used: fruit,
nut - oil, rind - tannic acid, leaves - used when young as vegetables. Time gathered: fruit - September/October, leaves - April
or May. Preparation: baked and salted they may replace almonds.
Medicinal: Water in hollows of beech cures scurf and scabby skin.
Eaten raw in large quantities (over ¼lb) they cause drunkenness.

HERB BENNET - Geum urbanum. Where found: common in ditches. Part
used: roots. Time gathered: all year round. Preparation: can
take the place of cloves as flavouring e.g. apples. Medicinal: a
small handful infused in a bottle of white wine for a week with a
piece of orange peel makes a very palatable vermouth.

BIRCH. Part used: Inner bark, raw or added in strips to soups
and stews. Sap - birch syrup - boil off water to thicken.

BISTORT. Part used: leaves and root. Preparation: soak leaves overnight in water before cooking. In Northern Europe a coarse flour is made.

BLUEBERRY. Part Used: leaves and fruits. Time gathered: Midsummer (Aug/Sept). Medicinal: blood purifyer, kidneys.

BURDOCK - Articum Lappa. Where found: common biennial roadside, waste ground. Part Used: Stalk (similar to asparagus), early leaves and roots, of first years growth. Time gathered: Spring - leaves and roots. Stems collected in midsummer. Preparation: stems as asparagus. Medicinal: Purifies blood, general tonic, good for rheumatism, gout & stone. Infusions made from root, seeds or leaves.

BUCK BEAN, MARSH OR WATER TREFOIL, BOGBEAN - Menydinthes trifoliata. Where found: marshes and bogs. Common. Part used: Roots herb. Time gathered: Spring. Preparation: powdered roots used in Lapland to make bread.

BULRUSH. Where found: Ponds and marshes. Part used: Roots and pollen. Preparation: dried ground roots - flour. "Dr. William Wilhering of Digitalis fame, related in the 18c. that the English poor used much of it in times of scarcity for their bread and broths." Eat the Weeds. B.C. Harris.

BLADDER CAMPION. Where found: meadows, waste places. Part used: Leaves (small). Time gathered: when 3 - 4" high. Preparation: cooked with other greens or in soup.

CATS-TAIL - Typha latifolia. Where found: marshes and wet places. Part used: upper parts of peeled young, golden pollen from mature cats tail - bread. Miniature leaves and white stalks are good munching. Every bit of the root except the skin is edible. Preparation: keep wet for easy peeling, removing fibre and pulping gives good flour. Very important plant, multi-use, yields of 140 tons per acre possible.

CHERVIL. Where found: common. Time gathered: Spring & Summer. Preparation: Salad & flavouring.

RUM CHERRY - Podus serotina. Where found: banks of brooks and rich woods. Part used: ripe fruits. Time gathered: August-September. Preparation: bitter. Eat uncooked or in sauce or jelly. Although there is no record of poisoning in man, the leaves and kernels of the fruit are poisonous - toxicity is higher in wet weather.

CHICKWEED. Where found: common in gardens and other cultivated land. Part used: Upper leaf portion. Time gathered: Early summer to late Fall. (With a thin cover of leaves, chickweed will live through winter and still be edible.) Preparation: eaten uncooked in salads. Medicinal: rich in iron.

CHICORY - Cichorium intybos. Where found: waste places, sandy soil, roadsides. Part used: roots, leaves (bitter unless blanched by earthing up). Time gathered: leaves - early spring, roots - summer. Preparation: leaves - salad, roots cooked as vegetable. Medicinal: stomach and kidney.

CLOVER - white, yellow or reddish flowers. Part used: flowers sucked for "honey." Early leaves. Roots after being smoked over a fire. Time gathered: leaves - Spring, blossom collected for drying when in full bloom. Mildly poisonous - mainly animals affected. Cyanogenetic/gycoside - yields prussic acid.

CLOUDBERRY - Rubus chamaemorus. Part used: red fruit. Preparation: excellent stewed or jammed.

COWBERRY - vaccivium vitis - idaea. Part used: berry.

COUCH GRASS. Where found: common. Part used: dried and ground roots and seeds.

WILD FOOD 2.

CRAB APPLE. Where found: naturalised in hedges, woods etc. Time gathered: September/October. Preparation: excellent jelly.

CRANBERRY - Where found: bogs. Part used: fruit.

DAISY - Bellis perennis. Where found: common, widespread. Part used: young roots until June.

DANDELION - Taraxacum officinale. Where found: common, widespread. Part used: leaves and roots (bitter unless earth blanched). Time gathered: particularly Spring, but all year round. Preparation: to remove bitter tang, boil in water just long enough to make it tender, especially roots. Medicinal: good for liver. 4 times the food value of lettuce - Eat the weeds!

DEWBERRY - Rubus caesius. Where found: common (similar to blackberry) hedges and thickets. Part used: fruit. Time gathered: August/September.

DULSE - Dilsea edulis (Rhodymenia palmata). Where found: very common seaweed. Time gathered: all year round. Preparation: may be eaten raw or boiled.

ELDER - Sambucus nigra. Where found: common, widespread. Part used: berries and flowers and young shoots. Time gathered: blossoms when not fully expanded, fruits when ripe. Medicinal: good for skin, every part has some use. Magic powerful - many legends.

FIREWEED. Part used: young stems, the young leaves make passable greens. Preparation: cook as asparagus.

(YELLOW) GOATS BEARD - Tragopogon pratense. Where found: waste places. Part used: tapering roots. Time gathered: Sept. - Nov. Preparation: steam. Similar to SALSIFY - tragopogon porrifolius. Rough grassy places chiefly S. England.

GOOSEBERRY - Ribes (Oxyacanthoides) uva-crispa. Where found: thick, wet woods. Part used: the fruits, leaves. Time gathered: leaves - spring, fruits - July/Aug. Preparation: leaves - salad or coleslaw. Medicinal: fever reducing.

GLASSWORT (beach asparagus) - salicornia perennis. Part used: whole. Preparation: boiled as a potherb, but finds its best flavor when pickled. Young plants - salad.

GRASSES. Where found: common. "All our British grasses with the exception of darnel are wholesome food." Mary T. Quelch. Time gathered: Cut young. Preparation: Boil until tender, serve as a green vegetable, or dry and crumble to powder, add to all sorts of food. Medicinal: See P.16-19 "Eat the Weeds". 12lb. of powdered grass has more vitamins than 340 lb. of vegetable and fruit. 25% of diet could be grass!?

HAZEL (NUT) - Carylus Americana. Where found: common, widespread. Part used: fruit - nut. Time gathered: September/October. Preparation: store in jar under ground 2 or 3 feet, cover nut with thick layer of salt. Fit tight-fitting cover. Medicinal: substitute for animal protein. Contents: Ca, Mg, Ph P, S Fat 64%, Protein 16.5%. Hazelrods used for water divining.

HAWTHORN - Crataegus species. Where found: common. Time gathered: early Autumn. Preparation: marmalade and preserve. Part used: Haws (fruits) Raw, Haws are a possible cause of poisoning.

HOPS - Humulus Lupus. Part used: young shoots, the fruits (stobiles). Time gathered: the shoots in Spring, the hops in early September. Preparation: shoots as asparagus or as a potherb N.B. shoots are given away in hop gardens, when the bines are pruned. At one time, ground hops were used as a substitute for baking powder.

HORSE CHESTNUT (no relation to the Sweet Chestnut). Where found: common, widespread. Part Used: leaves, bark and fruit. Time gathered: Sept/Oct (for nuts). Preparation: cannot be used as

WILD FOOD 3.

food without being processed commercially (method?) during W.W.II.
apparently tried and was uneconomical. High carbohydrate content.
Potentially useful. Fodder process: crush, soak overnight, boil
½ hour, strain, dried, husked and reduced to a meal. Medicinal:
various medicinal uses.

HORSERADISH - Amorcia rusticana. Where found: wet places, clay
soil. Part used: root and leaves. Time gathered: all year round.
Leaves - spring. Preparation: particularly good as a sauce.

HOREHOUND - Ballota nigra. Part used: infusion of whole plant.
Medicinal: sprigs in saucer with milk get rid of flies! Generally
use infusion to make candy.

IRISH MOSS, SALT ROCK MOSS, CARRAGEEN - Chondrus crispus. Time
gathered: April, May, wherever possible. Preparation: wash and
then bleach until white, dry until crisp. Store. Good for jellies and blancmange cooked with milk seasoned with vanilla extract or fruits. Medicinal: mixed with cucumber juice and/or
quince seed - hand lotion.

JUNIPER - juniperus communis. Where found: dry hills, limestone
areas. Part used: ripe fruits. Time gathered: August - October.
Preparation: quality flavoring, 2-4 berries per meal sufficient.
Possibly slightly poisonous at times - eat in moderation.

JAPANESE KNOTWEED - Polygamus cuspidatum. Where found: common on
waste ground (persistent garden escape). Part used: the young
shoots. Time gathered: In Spring when 6-8" high. Preparation:
steamed for 3-4 minutes.

COMMON KNOTGRASS, WILD BUCKWHEAT - Polygonum aviculare. Where
found: rich waste places, sides of brooks, common. Part used:
the closed flower heads contain the seeds. Time gathered: late
Summer when the flower head is completely pink. Preparation: the
seeds are dried and finely ground, used in biscuits etc. Possibly poisonous at times - eat in moderation. N.B. Beware the al-
lied Polygamun hydropiper - Water Pepper.

LADY SMOCK - Cardamine pratensis. Where found: damp meadows,
prolific. Part used: leaves. Time gathered: Spring-Autumn.
Preparation: leaves are peppery - hot. Young leaves may be used
in sandwiches. HAIRY CRESS - Cardamine hirsuta is similar but
milder growing in drier shady places.

LAMBS QUARTER, WILD SPINACH, PIGWEED, GOOSE FOOT - Cheropodium
album. Where found: rich soil, garden weed (indicator of a good
soil). Part used: stalks, leaves, flower and grains. Time gathered: young shoots when 5-6" high, fruit when mature but still
unopened. Preparation: raw and cooked. Young leaves raw. Rip-
ened fruits, completely dried, ground and used to prepare bread.
Highly Healthful.

WILD LETTUCE - Latuca scariola. Part used: the tender shoots
5-6" high. Time gathered: Spring. Preparation: steam, cook.
Possibly slightly poisonous at times, eat in moderation.

LICHENS. "Lichens are low, variously shaped, grey, brown or
black plants that are found throughout Northern Canada, and the
Arctic. They are edible." say the Canadian Mounties. Preparation: boiling or soaking in water to remove acidity. The "manna"
in the bible may have been the lichen - lecanora esculerilia.

LAUREL - Prunus Laurocerusus. Part used: small young leaf. Time
gathered: all year round. Preparation: delicate flavor, used as
a flavoring.

LAVER seaweed - Porphyra vulgaris. Purple and green varieties.
Time gathered: best gathered in March. Season: June-March. Preparation: boil for several hours or pickle. Chop and add to
stews. Rich in minerals.

LIME - Tilia (3 varieties). Where found: woods, limestone especially, various. Part used: flowers, sap, leaves. Time gathered: Summer. Preparation: tisane. Medicinal: Rich, healthful.

LIVE FOREVER - sedum purpureum. Where found: in woods, wet roadsides. Part used: leaves. Time gathered: Spring. Preparation: salad, coleslaw etc.

MARJORAM - Origanum vulgare. Part used: young leaf. Preparation: flavoring for soups and stews.

MARSH MARIGOLD - Caltha Palustris. Where found: in marshes and wet places, common. Part used: leaves and flower buds. Time gathered: Spring (when gethering, cut carefully near base with scissors, thus several crops will be obtained.) Preparation: Potherb as spinach - leaves. Early flower heads pickled are a substitute for capers. NEVER EAT UNCOOKED - contain Helleborin in the sap (aycoside.)

MARSH WOUNDWORT - Stachys palustris. Part used: young shoots (as asparagus roots tuberous.) Preparation: boil in water or there is an unappetising smell.

MEADOWSWEET - Pilipendula ulmaria. Where found: widespread. Damp places. Part used: leaf (aromatic). Medicinal: stomach upset and blood.

MUSTARD - Sinapis alba. Part used: young slightly peppery leaves enjoyed raw (also young yellow flowers) entire plant goes well cooked. Preparation: the ground seeds made into a paste with water make table mustard.

NASTURTIUMS. Where found: cultivated in gardens. Part used: young leaves and flowers, unripened seeds. Preparation: berries make pickle, flowers garnish, leaves - salad. Medicinal: good for skin. "A sluggish man should eat Nasturtium to arouse him from his torpidity." Pliny.

NETTLES - Urtica urens. Where found: widespread. Part used: heads and upper leaves. Time gathered: Spring and early Summer when 6-8" high. Preparation: steam for 2 minutes. Medicinal: drink nettle water when fasting. Nettle water for hair. Old nettle stems make cloth.

NIPPLEWORT - Lapsana communis. Part used: leaves. Time gathered: Spring and Summer.

PINE especially Lodge Pole Pine and White Pine. Part used: inner bark and fruits. Preparation: fresh or sun dried and ground up.

PIGNUT - Conopodium majus. Where found: in woods and shaded sides of fields. Part used: the tuber 2-3" below ground from the size of a pea to that of a hazlenut. Time gathered: June - September. Preparation: good boiled or baked.

PLANTAIN - Alisma plantaga. Part used: leaves. Preparation: cook in little water.

POPLAR - Populus nigra. Part used: inner bark/sap layer. Preparation: raw and cooked.

FIELD POPPY - papaver rhoeas. Part used: young leaves before plant flowers. Time gathered: May, June mostly.

PRIMROSE - Primula Vulgaris. Where found: waste places, roadsides, common in wood and shady banks. Part used: the young rosette of leaves and roots of the first years growth are gathered only in early Spring. Preparation: leaves - potherb, roots - soups. Possibly slightly poisonous at times - use with care.

PURSLANE - Lythrum portula. Where found: common on mud, especially acid soils. Part used: thick stems. Time gathered: throughout growing season. Preparation: best eaten uncooked or quickly steamed at most. Medicinal: "Cools the blood and causes appetite." Gerard.

EARLY PURPLE ORCHID - Orchis masalla. Where found: in shady
places - common. Part used: tubers. Time gathered: August. Preparation: baked until transparent, powdered to a fine powder. Substitute for cornflour.

QUINCE. Part used: fruit. Time gathered: late October. Preparation: preserves.

RAGWEED - Ambrosia artemissiaefolia. Where found: established on
waste ground though often only casual.

RAMSONS - Allium ursinum. Where found: woods, widespread, abundant in places. Part used: leaf (similar to garlic). Preparation:
as a garnish.

ROWAN, Mountain Ash - Sprbus aucuparia. Part used: crimson berries. Leaves poisonous. Preparation: jams and jellies.

SALSIFY - Tragopogan pornifolius. Where found: waste places usually by sea. Part used: root and young leaves (available through
winter).

SALAD BURNET - Poterium sanquisoba. Where found: common on downs
and dry pastures. Part used: young leaves. Time gathered:
Spring - Autumn. Preparation: salad or vinegar. Flavor similar
to cucumber.

SCARLET PIMPERNEL - Anagallis arvensis. Where found: common on
cultivated and waste land, dunes etc. Part used: seeds and
leaves. Time gathered: June collected herb must be handled with
care even when prepared as a tisane. Not really to be considered
an edible herb - mainly medicinal use. Medicinal: epilepsy and
feverish complaints/liver and dropsical conditions. Reported
poisoning, powerful. Use with care.

SEAWEEDS including: BLADDERWRACK, BLADDERLOCKS, TANGLE, GLASWORT,
DULSE, SEA KALE, KELP, LETTUCE LAVER. Many may be eaten as an
addition to meat, as pickle or as vegetable. Ploughed into land
fresh or composted, seaweed is excellent fertiliser. Can also
be used as cattle and sheep fodder. Soak in fresh water first.

SHEPHERDS PURSE - Capsella Bursapastaris. Where found: sandy,
waste places. Part used: leaves young. Fruits. Time gathered:
the leaves before herb flowers. Fruits before complete maturity.
Preparation: good in coleslaw. Medicinal: antiscubutic, stimu-
lant and divetic. Used in kidney complaints and dropsy.

SILVERWEED - Pontentilla anserina. Where found: common in waste
ground, roadsides and damp pastures. Part used: roots. Time
gathered: Spring, in the morning, keep cool, eat within 5 hours.
Preparation: steam 3-4 mins. in a little hot water. Tastes like
sweet parsnip. Medicinal: subsistence root.

SLOE - Prunus spinosa. Part used: fruit. Time gathered: Sept/
Oct. Preparation: stew slowly to extract flavor of kernels.

SLOKE - seaweed. Preparation: cook "indefinitely" (5 hours?)

SORREL - Rumex acetoselle. Where found: common herb, heaths and
acid soils (indicator of sour soil) sandy soils. Part used:
leaves fresh. Time gathered: whenever available. Preparation:
simmer for 10 minutes. Raw, take place of vinegar. Sometimes
poisonous when eaten in great quantity.

SUNFLOWER. Part used: seeds. Bud - pickle. "If you live in a
damp house, plant sunflowers against the outer walls and the damp
will disappear." Mary T. Quelch.

SWEET CHESTNUT. Where found: common, widespread. Part used:
fruit and leaves. Time gathered: fruit - October, leaves - June/
July. Should not be eaten raw due to tannic acid content. Medicinal: easily digested. Bread can be made from meal. Contains
Vit. K. therefore good for blood and circulation.

THISTLES. Where found: common. Parts used: receptacles on which florets are placed, boiled as artichokes, stalks when peeled are pleasant in salad or cooked as asparagus. Young shoots, young leaves and roots.

VIOLET - viola species. Where found: gardens, roadsides. Part used: leaves and flowers. Time gathered: Spring. Preparation: young leaves added to soups or in salad. Medicinal: bronchitis, chest, breathing.

TOUCH-ME-NOT - Impatiens noli-tangere. Where found: by streams, introduced elsewhere. Part used: early shoots less than 4-5" high. Time gathered: Spring to early Summer. Preparation: Always eat with other vegetables. Note. If too much of older part consumed, mild purgation may occur. Medicinal: high mineral content.

VALERIAN - Valerana officinalis. Where found: common, woods and grassy places. Part used: leaves, roots. Preparation: roots baked, leaves for tea.

WALNUT. Where found: rare out of cultivation. Part used: leaves, fruit, nuts. Time gathered: leaves - June - July. Fruit - Sept/ Oct. Preparation: leaves - infusions, fruits, nuts, walnut marmalade. Barks and skins. Green walnut have an outstandingly high vitamin C content. Skin healing and wound healing properties. Anti-toxic property.

WATERCRESS - Nasturtium officinale. Where found: gravelly, gently moving brooks. Part used: leaves. Time gathered: late Spring to early Summer. Do no gather if bottom is muddy. Preparation: never cook. Medicinal: antiscorbutic and stomach tonic. Very rich food.

WOOD SORREL - Oxalis acetosella. Where found: common in woods. Part used: leaves. Time gathered: Spring to Autumn. Preparation: used as replacement for vinegar.

TEAS & FLAVORINGS - HERBAL TISANES

Alfalfa	Chamomile	Hazel	Meadowsweet
Agrimony	Celandine	Horehound	Nettle
Avers	Chickweed	Honeysuckle	Primrose
Angelica	Cleavers	Hop	Plantain
Betony	Daisy	Ladys bedstraw	Samphire
Bilberry	Gorse leaf buds	Lime	Tansy
Bindweeds	Hawthorn	Lily of the Valley	Wild Thyme
Burnet	Holly	Marjoram	Wild Rose

Note : Gleaning from arable crops is not to be ignored. Mechanical reapers and gatherers will leave much on the ground. We collected over one cwt. of potatoes in about one hour from a small newly harvested field.

Data recently provided by Professor Brymour Thomas and others have shown that some weeds are much richer in the major mineral nutrients than normal fodder grasses, and may contain the trace elements in surprisingly large amounts. eg. Willowherb, Buttercup, Rosebay, Tufted vetch and Ribwort are rich in cobalt, Dandelion, Ribwort, Thistle and Stinging nettle are rich in copper. Yellow Rattle in manganese. Chicory Ribwort, Yarrow, Sainfoin and Salad Burnet in magnesium. Stinging nettle, Dandelion, Way Bread, Crosswort, Creeping Thistle and Chicory in iron.

whilst not owning land   by supplanting wild food
it is possible to obtain a food supply
growth to produce a balanced diet and a regular supply. First
it is necessary to assess the dietary value and availability
of wild food. Positions of useful species could be
marked on a map of the area you are living in. This
catchment area could be a small
town or a nomadic route across the
country. Suitable symbols may be used   for
important species and notes made of quantities likely
to be obtainable. These quantities are then added to a yearly
calendar so you can see what is available when. Account should
be taken of the possibilities of drying or otherwise preserving
large crops.   From this information and
a quantitive and dietary assessement of personal needs;
(depending on energy and growth requirements.)
)It may be calculated how much planting
of what types of foodplants, for cropping
at particular times must be undertaken.
Plantings will utilise odd unused pieces   of
land such as hedgerows, copses, derelict
house gardens. Species   for planting
are chosen to be inconspicuous
either because they are
common in the wild. eg.
dandelion & Good King Henry.
or because the edible part
is not very obvious
eg. root crops. Several
different types could be
sown on each 'site' by
either broadcasting
or seed drilling in
curving rows that
will not be easy
to discern as the work of a human
gardener.   It may be
necessary to suppliment the
diet with meat. For example you
could introduce fish into the
local pond and make sure
they are kept well fed
and   the pond is
kept clean.
The propagation of
wild fowl may be
encouraged along
with this pond operation.
You may be in a bleak
region or have very little
time, if so a staple such as
rice or potatoes or other grain may
have to be bought in bulk to suppliment
the gathered diet.   In summary:—
you need   1. A map showing wild food
species. 2. Quantities likely to be
obtainable at different seasons.
3. Food requirements
for three people
4. necessary additional
planting proposed.
(entrancing blend)
Unite! and
Disperse in Unity.

DISINTEGRATED FARM

A restricted number of animal species are at present reared for meat. Others are not only edible but of good flavour and are adaptable to rearing. Species can be selected whose eating habits would enable presently unusable areas of vegetation to be cropped; for instance the giraffe is able to crop tree tops.

It is interesting that the meat production in a wild game reserve is often greater than that in a comparable area which is farmed. This is due to mixed species of wild animal having complimentary diets and other habits. There could be mixed species farming and intensive wild life management as part of a better planned use of food resources.

Urban rearing of animals such as rabbits, chickens, dogs, goats & fishes could solve some of the waste disposal problems. Feed can consist of a large amount of table scraps, and make use of waste plot weeds, grass and greengrocers' green vegetable trimmings ──────────.

L'UMBRIA ILLUSTRATA
PERUGIA - La gran fiera del 4 Maggio   TILLI - PERUGIA 324

REARING ANIMALS

To obtain an unbroken supply of milk the year round you must have two cows. Cow grasing is good for the soil and they do little damage to trees. One of the Channel Island breeds is usually more docile and therefore easier to man-age on a small holding. Pedigree cows are the best to get, but you will probably only be able to afford an old cow. Seek advice from an experienced herdsman when deciding which breed or cross to buy. When buying an expensive cow have a veterinary examination made.

Housing: minimum size for a shed is 8ft. x 15ft., but should be bigger, having in addition an adjoining food store and dairy. Cows are best tied up with chains.

Food: Spring and summer grasses provide the best food for cows; an acre per cow. A second ½ acre will be sown to give sufficient hay even in the worst years. A quarter of an acre should be oats and beans mixed; a quarter of an acre for kale and swedes.

Insemination: artificial is the normal practice for smallholders unless you can entice a local bull.

Calving: A cow should have at least six weeks rest from milking before she is due to calve again. Throughout spring and summer cows do better if allowed to calve outdoors. The calf is fed the mothers milk for the first week or so; then a proprietary calf meal.

In an average lactation a cow gives 600-800 gallons (ie. approx one year.) Two cows may be kept on a minimum of 2 acres.
460 gallons milk = 200 lbs butter
+ 200 gals. skim milk
+ butter milk.
460 gallons milk = 200 lbs cheese

It is best to buy a goatling, in kid, from a good milking strain. If you buy a goat in milk go to see her on two consecutive milkings which will give a good idea of what she is actively producing. The udder is the most important guide, when milked out it should feel like a ball of silk. The nature of the soil plays a great part in the health of a goat. Avoid damp marshy land; a chalk subsoil is best.

Goats need a good shed (about 8ft. sq. for two goats.) There should be south facing windows to make full use of the winter sun when the goats will be confined to their stalls. The best method of grazing out goats is to tether them near a small portable shed in which they can shelter during storms. (not being as hardy as cows.)

concentrates: important for milkers, might include linseed cake, flake maize, a good sample of winter oats and broad bran. Root crops and greens must be clean. Hay is the principle food.
Those who cannot grow their own hay could find a lot of valuable food growing wild on country roadsides and hedge ways or derelict town sites. Stinging nettles, docks, many herbs and hedge clippings can be dried and stored for winter which helps give necessary variety to their diet when other foods are scarce. With limited land resources it is best to stall feed with a yard for excercise; the land being used to grow feed crops. Anything likely to damage udders such as brambles or poisonous plants should be removed from the pasture area.

Breeding: the season lasts from Sept. to Feb. Period of pregnancy is about 150 days; Although there is not usually much trouble at birth it is important to find out about care of the goat during pregnancy.

Lactation period is up to one year long. You may expect to obtain 200 gallons of milk per year from on average goat.

MILKERS

Rabbits may be kept in a comp-
-aratively small space and be
maintained to a considerable extent
on waste products from the garden
or allotment. Green food for a few
animals can usually be obtained for
the labour involved in collecting it
from 'the wild'. Rabbits are worth
keeping for their flesh and fur,
while their manure is of value to
the soil. They are particularly suited
to keeping in the town back-yard.

A Rabbit thrives on a balanced
daily diet of food equal to 2 oz per
one lb of its live weight. It will eat
a very wide range of food including
_____ the leaves and twigs of
nearly all deciduous trees, dried
nettles, brambles, potato parings,
dandelion, clover, etc. Concentrates
are added in the ratio of 1 : 5.
e.g. mix bran 6 parts, barley meal
2 parts + white fish meal one part.
Every type of table scrap may be
used, even orange peel and tea
leaves, as basic feed.

Pedigree rabbits of the best
known breeds are just as hardy
and prolific as their humbler
relations and will provide fine fur
or in the case of the Angora breed
beautifully soft wool.

✳ Legal Note on Animal Keeping.
Anyone is at liberty to keep, on his
own premises, any animal he chooses
So long as it is not a nuisance to his
neighbour. A 'nuisance' is something
which interferes with the neighbours
reasonable enjoyment of his own
property. What is 'reasonable'
depends on time and place to great
measure; but if you want to keep
chickens in the middle of the city
some diplomacy will be necessary!

Young pullets may be bought
3—6 months old if you want to
avoid the extra time and accomod-
-ation spent in breeding and rearing
There is no reason why a few chickens
shouldn't be kept in towns; the best
breeds being bantams such a Sebright
or Leghorns.

Keep the nest-boxes very clean—
fresh straw every week and a
dusting with a good insect powder.
The houses should be whitewashed
inside 2 or 3 times a year.

Table scraps with equal parts of
bran and middling will give them
good feeding with some green scraps
and a handful of grain per bird.

Birds for the table are penned in a
small place for about a fortnight before
being killed and fed on mashes of
oats and barley with some added
fat if possible. No grain or grit is
given during this period. Before
killing the bird is starved for 24 hours.

Ducks of a good laying breed and
strain usually begin to lay when
about 5 months old and continue
to lay at least one season longer
than hens. Breeding of Ducks in
a small space is not advisable,
although some of the smaller laying
varieties will breed without access
to water.   Stock should be kept in
active condition by giving only suffi-
-cient food to suppliment their own
foraging. Adult ducks need only one
feed daily for about 8 months of the
year. Diet suppliment may be allowed
when a large no. of eggs for cons-
-umption is required.
Ducks and ducklings must have dry
bedding but no other special accom-
-odation is necessary.

Note: Geese are even more self-
-reliant than ducks.

Pork is to be found as a principle food of most peoples in the earlier stages of sedentary civilisation; from the South Pacific to the English shire. Swine multiply quickly, herd together and generally don't need much looking after.

"It is advisable to start with a newly weaned pig about 8 weeks old of a breed popular in your area. Above all, get an animal with a vigorous constitution; a greedy lusty fellow, active on his legs, lengthy and round in shape, with a clean and pliable skin covered with a fine coat of glossy hair."

Apart from the standard feed of roots, vegetables and meal, a young pig may pick over grass from the wayside, garden weeds, acorns and similar found foods. Various food processing and canteen wastes may also be used. A newly weaned pig usually requires 2lb of food per day which goes up to 6lb at 6months. If carefully fed from the start a pig should weigh from 170-180lb live weight when about 6 months old. The pig is then old enough to kill.

Pigsty: 15ft x 18ft will provide enough accomodation for two sows. The covered portion is 6ft from front to back. Often this may be simply built as a lean-to onto an existing structures.

Note: before starting consult the local sanitary regulations regarding pig keeping; it is very unlikely that a piggery would be welcome within or adjacent to a town.

Beekeeping must not be assessed by the value of its honey only. Fertilisation of crop, within the radius of flight of about 2 miles, is the most important factor.

February is the beginning of the honey harvest. The Queen begins to lay her eggs and the worker bees can be seen on the crocuses and snowdrops during the sunny periods. There is no more beautiful scene than to watch the bees coming home to their hives carrying all the different colours of pollen which they collect from every flower, herb, tree and shrub that blooms. The man who makes the successful beekeeper is one who observes the action of the bees outside the hive, and so learns what is going on inside.

equip-ment: when several hives are to be kept, standardisation of equip-ment is a great help as then parts are interchangeable. One of the chief reasons for swarming is overcrowding——allow the queen two brood boxes to lay her eggs in.

A swarm of about 5lb is best for the beginner; bought in may. "The chief attributes for the good handling of bees are knowledge of the habits of the bee, firm but gentle movements, adequate protection of the manipulator and proper subjugation of the bees." Adequate protection may be as simple as a veil for the face.

Honey will be taken off and ext--racted at the beginning of July.

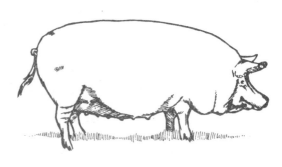

BEE & PIG

FISH FARMING

Origins: For many years now people have been farming fish. It is said, the Chinese were the first to tend fish on a large scale followed by the Romans. The self-sufficient monasteries of the Middle ages developed sophisticat- -ed carp ponds that would figure prominently in their economy.

The river stocking of Salmon, Trout and the like are large scale operations and will not concern us here. The small lake or pond seems to be a more realistic immediate proposition for those interested in starting Pisciculture.

Ponds: Muddy, stagnant pools will never provide fish of good taste. Control, of leaves falling into the water and the build up of mud through over many water plants, is necessary. (the removed muck will often serve very well to enrich the soil of the vegetable garden.) Ponds must be kept as clean as possible; and no more weed should be permitted to accumulate in them than is just sufficient for the shelter and the production of food for the fish.

It is best to have two, three or more ponds communicating by hatches with one another so that when one is drained, the others may remain full, and each or all of them may be raised or let down at pleasure. One or other is usually drained and left dry for some months every year or two. Some weeds are indispensable as they harbour food, serve to aerate and keep pure the water and are needed for the fish to spawn amongst. The Water Crowsfoot is one of the most useful weeds for ponds.

Ponds should be cleared of fish once in every 3 or 4 years, they do not pay if left for longer intervals. A few pairs of the larger fish should be left as breeders with whatever fry may exist, but the middle sized fish should be taken out. That is fish from 2-5 lbs. Carp, for example, grow slowly above 5 or 6 lbs and take up more space than is worthwhile.

Ponds that have rookeries beside them have been found not to be much of a success. The reason for this is that the dropping of the Rooks, which are very considerable, contain a large percentage of lime, which seems to be bad for the fish.

Best fish for ponds are Carp, Tench, Jack and Bream. It is always well, even in carp and Tench ponds to have a few brace of Jack amongst the carp and Tench for the purpose of keeping the fry down, so that they do not devour to much of the food from the larger fish. The proportions recommended by Mr. Boccius, who is an authority upon this subject, are 200 brood carp, 20 brood tench + 20 brood Jack, to the acre; best time for stocking being the end of October.

Mirror Carp are particularly esteemed. Eels are to be discouraged as they tend to devour the spawn. Duck, Swans or fancy waterfowl also tend to reduce spawn. Perch thrive fairly in some ponds but not in others, as they rapidly get the muddy flavour so common to English pondfish. If a pond has a good stream running through it trout are possibly the best choice. Gudgeon will do well in ponds.

extracted notes from FISH-CULTURE
by Francis Francis 1865.

Nowadays an artificial aquatic ecosystem may be designed to produce fish flesh in the shortest time with the least waste. Newton Harrisons 'Portable Fish farm' reprinted in Architectural Design magazine 11/71 has 6 tanks (20'x 6'x 2') of butyl rubber. 3 tanks hold catfish at various stages of growth; the other tanks hold oysters, Lobsters and shrimp resp- -ectively. The fish eat grain and fruit. Catfish entrails are fed to the Lobsters. The oysters and shrimp feed on cultured Algae Dunaliella. The algae feed on 1 tablespoonful of Potassium nitrate, 1 tablespoonful citus growers mix, which contains iron salts and other trace metals and 4 oz of fish based liquid plant food. The chemicals are produced by the humans who eat the catfish, lobsters, oysters and shrimps.

PISCICULTURE

FISH FARMING

INDOOR APPARATUS.

THE Catchers Art... From the "Fifteenth Book of Natural Magic" by J.B. Porta, published in 1658, the reader may learn how to allure and take living creatures by meat, whistle, light, smell, love and other frauds, or else to make them drunk and take them, or to kill them with venom.

For example, stags and boars are taken with a pipe. Nets being pitched and all things made ready for to ensnare them, a man that can play well on the flute goes through dales and hills and woods and plays as he goes, near their haunts. They listen exceedingly after it and are easily taken by it, for they are so ravished that they forget where they are ———————

Hawking

HUNTING.

Sporting rights are a form of private property,
and can only be assigned by deed duly signed
and sealed. Like all property, they are rigidly
protected by law.

Paying sporting rights is the only solution.

In most places you need either a licence or permission.
There are restrictions on seasons and size of take.

Fishing can constitute an important part of
sporting rights.

You need to know about local laws and seasons.

Rabbits, hares and some birds, rather than being treated as pests, can be 'ranched' and thus supply useful animal protein, high in the amino acid Lysine, which is at too low a level in cereals.

Bradford Angier reckons that hunting is the best way of living off the country and being sure of getting a full range of your food requirements. He is referring to North America; but the same goes for this country altho' your choice of beast is limited, in most cases, to small game such as the rabbit, squirrel and pigeon. The generally used weapon in this country seems to be the 12 bore shotgun. Any gun user should become expert before using it in open country and will need a police license. Another piece of equipment, that Angier lays stress on, is the usefulness of binoculars in serious hunting. Also see catapult section.

The Common Squirrel.

A diet of lean meat only, such as Rabbit, will lead to digestive upset and then to starvation as fat is absolutely essential in a carnivore diet. Fresh fatty meat however is a complete diet even with nothing else.
Overcooking generally lowers the nutritional value. So cook only to make palatable (ie. tasty) or to kill germs.

The Sparrow.

Adult rabbits depend so much on camouflage that if you pretend not to see one you may be able to come close enough to make a thrown rock and quick follow up grab effective.

Nearly every part of the victim animal is edible. Aboriginies pulp small creatures up and put the lot into a pot.

Blood, which is not so different from milk, is rich in easily absorbed vitamins and minerals. Don't waste it Fresh blood may be secured and carried in a bag improvised from a part of the entrails.
Mineral rich bone marrow should not be forgotten.

The Hare.

Rabbits are very easy to clean. Beginning an opening in the loose skin of the back, with a knife, tear the fragile skin apart around the body. Then peel the skin off inside out, forward and backward, cutting off the extremities. i.e. head, tail and feet. The entrails are then dropped out by opening just below the ribs with the knife. Save the heart and liver from the entrails.

The Dodo.

150 types of birds and animals have become extinct through human actions. 1000 species are in danger or rare.

Labyrinthodon salamandroides (restored).

SNARE

Scaring predators from their kill may provide fresh meat, Not uncommonly a hawk that has caught something rather awkward to lift such as a partridge or hare. The fox may provide a similar chance. In a tight spot Gamebirds such as grouse may be bagged with only sticks and stones.

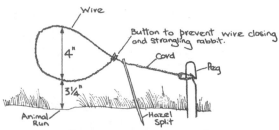

Wire
Button to prevent wire closing and strangling rabbit.
4"
Cord
Peg
3¼"
Animal Run
Hazel Split

Insects of all kinds are very good food; being mainly fat they are a concentrated food and you do not need so very many to keep you alive. The only common insect said to be unpalat- -able are ants which are bitter because of their formic acid content; however Aborigines have a method of preparing them with berries to make a sort of Lemonade.

The Hedgehog : a traditional Romany delicacy. Easy to catch, it is baked in clay which retains the sharp quills. However, the Hedgehog is a beneficial animal...........

Grey Squirrels are said to damage young forest trees.(I.e. in great numbers they are a pest) and are also very good prepared en casserole.

DEAD FALL

Dragonflies, Moths, Mayflies etc. may all be eaten if the natural western revulsion to creepy-crawlers can be overcome.

Lizards and Snakes are considered by many peoples as a delicacy.

The Garden Snail, Helix aspera was once eaten in large numbers in Bristol.

Traps are best set with gloved hands and arranged in exact mimicry of their surroundings.

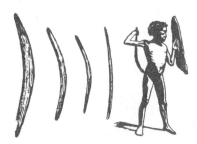

The Italian version of toad-in-the- -hole is made with small birds baked in palenta. The birds used could probably be the common local pest; For example the sparrow.

Other animals may be trained to hunt for you; examples being the ferret and the Hawk. How does one go about training such an animal?

Birds fed with grain fermented or soaked in alcohol are easily caught.

Disguising the features has advantages in hunting in open country. To help the hunter approach within range of accuracy of his weapon.
A mask representing a harmless animal can be used to allay the suspicions of his prey.

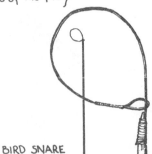

BIRD SNARE from TIERRA DEL FUEGO

CATAPULT.

The Catapult, though comparatively a modern invention, has attained wonderful popularity, and few indeed must there be of our young readers who have not possessed, or at least used, one of these simple but effective weapons, which for accuracy, handiness, and general capabilities may be fairly said to rank only next to firearms. Indeed, against small fry such as rats, the smaller birds, and even squirrels--that is to say, for the general requirements of a boy --they may be made, in skilful hands, even more effective ; for, while scarcely less deadly, they are inconspicuous and quite noiseless, and so quite make up for any deficiency in certainty of execution by giving the young sportsman more and better chances than he would get if his game were alarmed at the sound or even the sight of a gun.

Another advantage they possess, too, over firearms, which should not be overlooked : they are not dangerous to their possessors, and need not be so to other people. In London, indeed, and most large towns, their use is forbidden in the streets, but so are hoops and many other toys which are perfectly harmless in their place ; in the country they are, of their kind, as safe as anything a boy can have.

Catapults are now to be procured cheaply at any toy-shop, but they may be made at home much more efficiently with very little trouble. Get a forked stick, the shape of the letter Y, about six or seven inches in length, the prongs about two inches apart. To the extremity of each of these prongs lash securely a strip of strong india-rubber spring about six inches in length, and attach the loose ends of these springs to an oval piece of soft leather, 1½ inches long by an inch in width, whipping them carefully and strongly for a distance of nearly an inch ; this oval forms a kind of pocket in which to place the missile.

The most useful ammunition is duck-shot ; clay marbles do very well, and even gravel-stones at a pinch may be made to do good service ; but the first-named are preferable in every way, for range, accuracy, penetration, and

500 SHOT AUTOMATIC SLINGSHOT

Only $1.75 plus 25¢ pp & hd.

Cracks like a rifle when it hits. Ideal for small game or target firing. At a glance you know how many shots remain in magazine. Tremendous power in lbs. per inch. Pure gum rubber slings. Automatic reloading action. Just press the button and fire again. Lets you get off as many as 3 shots even at a moving target. Fits pocket. Free Starting load. . . . BARGAIN CO.—Sling Dept—8-OLS, 1 Park Ave., New York, N.Y. 10016.

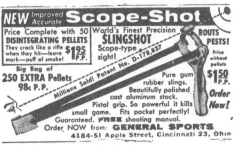

NEW Improved Accurate **Scope-Shot**

Price Complete with 50 DISINTEGRATING PELLETS
They crack like a rifle when they hit—leave mark—puff of smoke! $1.25 P.P.

Big Bag of 250 EXTRA Pellets 98¢ P.P.

World's Finest Precision **SLINGSHOT** Scope-type sight!

Millions Sold! Patent No. D-179,837

ROUTS PESTS!

Price without pellets

Pure gum rubber slings. Beautifully polished cast aluminum stock. Pistol grip. So powerful it kills small game. Fits pocket perfectly! Guaranteed. FREE shooting manual.

$1.50 P.P.

Order Now!

Order NOW from: **GENERAL SPORTS** 4184-SI Apple Street, Cincinnati 23, Ohio

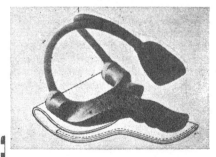

SLING SHOT offset handle of lightweight epoxy, molds into shooter's hand. Use of 30 lb. surgical tubing as hookup, doubles speed of missile. Shoots ½ oz. slug through ¼ in. plywood. Fully guaranteed. State which hand, left or right. $3.50. The Sling Shot is available with holster at $5.95 ppd. Boler Mfg., Dept. SA-12, Box 1182, Winnipeg, Manitoba, Canada.

ANGLER

The amount of regular anglers in this country is likely to be around quarter of a million which far out-weighs any other hunting activity. I will here consider a few simple methods of fishing and some of the more tasty fish that may be commonly caught.

Rod and Line Techniques. The rod may be almost any reasonably long light strong pole, however a well made split cane or fibreglass rod with the proper attachments to guide the line and hold the reel in place will only cost a few pounds in the fishing shop which exists in almost every town. The line may be any fine cord or string but modern nylon line is almost invisible. At 60p — 100p for 100yds length depending on strength — well worthwhile.

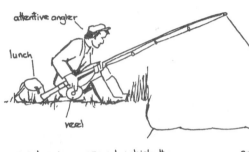

attentive angler

lunch

reel

The mechanism around which the line is wound and regulated is known as the reel and again they are reasonably cheap new and secondhand. Ask your local dealer to show you the various types of this basic equipment and tell you how they operate. You should be able to get enough equip-ement to start fishing for between £1 and £5.

Float Fishing : A small float of something like cork, quill, plastic or wood is used to suspend the bait at a chosen depth. The float, which is weighted with small leads so it is only just above the water, will indicate when the fish takes the bait by bobbing up and down and finally sliding away under water. This action stimulates the adrenalin glands of the angler, who brings his rod up swiftly but not too hard to secure the hook in the fishes' mouth without causing grievous bodily harm. The fish is then gradually brought to shove using the reel. Considerable skills are involved in chasing the time and place, bait, casting into the best spot, choosing the right depth and so on.
Floats may be simply home-made from many materials.

Ledgering. By this method the bait is kept at a particular place on the bottom by the use of a weight.

coffin lead

stop lead clipped to line

line to rod taut

line to hook loose

bait

When the fish takes the bait the line becomes taughter and this is indicated by various devices either spontaneously invented, learnt or bought.

Live Bait. Used to catch carnivorous fish. A small live fry is caught and attached to the hook in such a way as to keep it as lively as possible. A larger than usual float is used. Considered by some to be cruel. The alternative is to use an artificial live bait.

fine nylon line

float

small weights bring float upright

hook with bait

prey

Spinning. A device which when drawn through the water imitates a young fish. Used as an alternative to live bait to catch the carnivorous fish species. The technique involves casting 'the spinner' out a considerable distance and then slowly reeling it in so that it looks like a feeble young fish.

this part is silver and wobbles, flashing when drawn through water.
With a little skill spinners may be fab-ricated at home. This is a useful skill as many carnivores like weeds so that spinners are easily lost.

Flyfishing. A special rod and line are required to cast the small imitation fly into the likely spot. Apparently not as skilled or difficult as it looks.

FISHING

For Anglers methods of fishing other than rod and line are generally thought of as unsportsmanly; but when fishing for food different ethics apply. However take care not to overfish a water without restocking.

Netting : Unless you have enough net to seal off the fishes escape, by throwing a net across a stream or entrance of a bay, the net should be trawled in a wide and deep arch perhaps between two boats.

Spearing : One procedure is to thrust the spear very slowly through the water toward the target, often to within inches of the fish before making the final jab.
A torch at night will attract fish and they may then be speared.
An arrow tethered by a thin light cord may also be used.

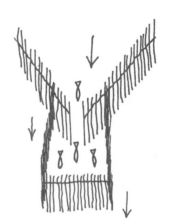

Electrical fishing : The apparatus consists of a generator giving a direct current of about 250 volts between two electrodes. A catch net is, if possible, drawn across the river below the apparatus. When the current is turned on it has the effect of lining up fish, in the vicinity, between the electrodes. The fish then swim mesmerised toward the positive terminal which may take the shape of a landing net. Left on long enough a strong current will knock the fish out. No damage occurs to fish caught in this manner so it is good for restocking.

Poisoning : Lime thrown onto a pool will bring fish helpless to the surface. Many herbal fish narcotics are used by primitive peoples.

Catching animals by hand is surp- -risingly easy if you have the art. A friend of mine purposefully killed a large fish, that was basking in the shallows, with a large rock.
Large trout may be obtained by 'tickling'. That is moving the submerged hand slowly towards the fish and then gently caressing it whilst man- -oeuvring into a position in which you can grasp it firmly. A method traditionally favoured by English poachers.
memo. Meat tastes better and lasts longer if the animal is killed instantly without being frightened or struggl -ing.

The Coracle : still used for fishing in South Wales. This sketch is taken from a painting by George Delamotte. 1818.

FISHING 2.

BAIT.

The Perch: easily recognised by the stripes across its body. It is a very common fish all over the British Isles in every kind of water. Worms or small fish are the best bait for large Perch, although small Perch up to one half pound will take almost anything. Perch is said to be one of the best fish from the culinary point of view, especially if coming from running water or gravelly lakes. Its flesh is firm and white, without the muddy tang which accompanies many freshwater fish. It is usually good whether it is fried, grilled or steamed.
Note: take care in handling the Perch as the spines on its dorsal fin and those on its gill covers can cause unpleasant injury.

SPRING.—p. 15.

The Pike: A voracious carnivore caught by spinning or on live bait. Common in all localities it is a lone fish not found in shoals. Isaac Walton the famous fisherman and poet described the medium sized Pike of a few pounds as 'a dish of meat too good for any but anglers or very honest men'.

The Trout: they live in the faster, cleaner rivers of Britain. Being of delicate taste and good sport they are often protected heavily and a license may be necessary. They are angled for with fly or by spinning. Fly fishing needs some skill but it is not the hopelessly difficult art it is commonly thought. Special equipment in the form of a whippy rod and weighted line are needed but are no more expensive than coarse fishing tackle.

Tench, Carp, Roach, Dace, Bream, Gudgeon may be taken on small worms, bread paste and crust, hemp seed, maggots, boiled wheat and barley. They are all reasonable to eat although often taste rather muddy if no spices are used in cooking.

As seashore fish are mostly bottom feeders similar baits will do for a whole variety of fish. The major exception is spinning usually for mackerel or bass.
There was a report in the Angling Times of someone who caught a flounder on a piece of orange peel; white plastic drinking cups are regularly found in the stomachs of South coast cod. However the main baits used are :——

Worms: the species normally used by sea anglers are lugworms and ragworms, both have accounted for almost every species of sea-fish. You can buy them at tackle shops or dig them for yourself in sandy or muddy beaches at low tide. Care should be taken of marshy ground or quickly rising tides.

Fish Baits: Almost any fish flesh can be used but herring and mackerel are best because of the oily nature of their flesh. Use strips of flesh when going for small species, and fillets, halves or even wholes when going for big Tope, Skate, Conger and Sharks. Squid, although not actually fish, is also a popular bait.

Shellfish: Crabs, mussels, razorfish, limpets, cockles, clams and prawns can be good bait in the right locality. Ask the local fishermen. These baits may all be collected at low tide.

A Bait for All Fish
"Take of the strong whale, eight drachms; yellow butterflies, anniseed, cheese of goats milk, each of four drachms; of opoponax two drachms, hogs blood four, as much galbanum.
Pound them all together and pour on sour wine. Make cakes and dry them in the sun."
'15th Book of Natural Magic
J.B. Porta. 1658.'

FISH BAIT

PERCH.—*Perca fluviátilis.*

TROUT.—*Salmo fario.*

ROACH.—*Leuciscus rútila.*
BREAM.—*Abramis brama.*
TENCH.—*Tinca vulgáris.*

SPECIES

Ponds integrate in many ways into
the human ecosystem. Water can
be used as a heat transference
medium, heat sink, humidity
controller, energy storage via
hydroelectric generation, tran-
sport system (floating, rotating
solar tracking house) as well as
things such as suggested in the
fish farming section.

Anyone with a half acre or larger
homestead should be able to build
and maintain a successful fish
pond, regardless of his resources
or geography. The easiest method
of making a pond is by damming a
small valley fed by a small
spring or artesian well. However,
most people, not lucky enough to
be in this position, will have
to excavate.

One of the poorest places to
excavate your pond is in a
gravel or sandy soil which will
not hold the water, and will
need to be sealed. This can be
done with strips of heavy black
polythene laid to completely
cover the bottom and sides. The
strips should be lapped about
3" to form a seal. 'Sand ponds'
can also be sealed with clay
if it is available. The sides
are water-proofed by digging
a narrow trench one foot deeper
than the pond and 3 feet outside
its water area. This trench
which surrounds the pond is
then tamped full of clay. The
bottom is sealed by throwing
clay into the water, and stirring up well so that as they
clay particles settle, they will
form a tight and long lasting
seal.

If a tamped earth dam is used to
contain water, care must be taken
that a proper spill way is constructed to avoid erosion.

Digging a pond by hand is slow,
laborious work, so if you can
somehow persuade someone to lend
you a tractor, mounted backhoe
or other excavator..........
or you can rent one if you know
how to drive it, offering your
pond site as a "demonstration
pitch" for an earth moving con-
tractor might work! Another
method is by blasting, but a
skilled operator is necessary.

Note on Use of Earth. The soil
dug from a fish pond may (unless
grossly unsuitable) be used to
build a house, barn or wall.
(see Vol. 1. Shelter). The top
soil removed, may be used on
poor pastures with thin soil.
The subsoil may be used to
landscape areas, creating pro-
tective hillocks.
Thinking of your operation as
a whole ecological subsystem
within the global ecosystem
things begin to fit together.

When the excavation is done,
the next consideration is getting enough water to fill it
and keep it filled.

Methods of filling and keeping
full.

1. Stream.

2. Well.

3. Roof runoff from all available buildings.

4. Construct local drainage
leading into the pond. Works
only if the pond has enough
reserves to last through the
dry season.

Stocking

Your local pet shop aquaria will
be able to tell you of your nearest source of fish. Or you can
attempt to catch your own sprats.
Also salmon and trout fisheries
often weed out coarse fish and
sell cheap.

✻ An intensively managed pond, is
one in which the fish are carefully fed and kept to a good
number.

✻ Food plants such as cattail may
be planted around the pond.

✻ Aeration of a small still pond
is important and a covering of
ice in winter may cause your
fish to die of oxygen starvation. A simple remedy for this,
is to have an aerating wind
pump rigged up near the pond.

FOOD is not always convenient in its primary state. It may be inaccessible, unavailable, quick to go bad, unable to be chewed, poisonous, not easily digested and so on. For instance in some situations weight and bulk of food may be the primary consideration...

Back packing weights
Short distances (portages)......75 lbs total
Day long hiking ....35 lbs total

Of the continuous hiking weight of 35 lbs. as much as 20 lbs could be food, the rest of the weight being taken by other essential survival gear. Two day rations for one man on a relaxed hike can weigh between 2½ - 3 lbs so a man can eat properly for about a week from backpacked food if water is freely available and the going is easy.

One pound of dessicated eggs is equivalent to some five dozen fresh eggs.
One pound of whole milk powder makes eight pints of liquid whole milk.
Drying is a process that loses few nutrients ———————

TWO WOMEN GRINDING AT THE MILL.—LUKE XVII. 35: MATT. XXIV. 41.

PROCESS

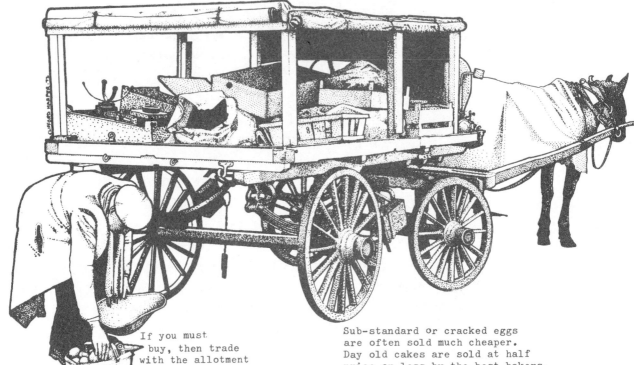

If you must buy, then trade with the allotment locals and others who grow their own food. Buying direct from small growers, it is likely that you will hear the life history of your shopping from seed.

For those who require pure food, or rather, who are prepared to travel to get pure food, "The Whole Food Finder" published by Henry Doubleday and the Soil Association, is invaluable, giving names and addresses of the most reputable organic growers. There is also "The Organic Food Service" directory of organic growers and produoers 5p from The Organic Food Service, Ashe, Churston Ferrers, Brixham, S. Devon. Buying from such sources will support their worthy effort to grow food without harmful chemicals.

Buying in Bulk. of course saves money, and means you don't have to go shopping every day/week for the same staples.

Sub-standard or cracked eggs are often sold much cheaper. Day old cakes are sold at half price or less by the best bakers. Fetes and bazaars usually have home-made foods cheap, and its a nice atmosphere to be shopping in.

Cash and Carry can often get things in bulk much cheaper. Indian and other specialist food shops will often make personal arrangements for bulk buying. Trade food markets, such as Covent Garden are very nice at dawn. Organise your friends, who eat like you, and buy bulk for 50-100 people really cheap, but you have the problem of money collecting -

(digger!)

Take the trouble to find your nearest small-time bakery and the baking times - talk to the baker, encourage him to make more basic bread, but better still, grind your own bulk bought grain and bake your own. The best way to ensure plenty of regular callers is to bake your own bread!

BUYING.

A CHILIAN GREENGROCER.

Broken biscuits are cheap food.
Pet Shops - wheat, grain.

Markets

Diplomatic, skilled and well timed "market gleaning" will provide regular free food in London. It is more difficult to get regular free food by this method in provincial towns.

Methods: picking up stuff thats rolled into the gutter or thats been thrown out because its a bit off, or asking stall-holders for food thats overripe etc. Either arrive early for the sorting out, or late for the chuck out.

Greengrocers

Supermarkets throw out hygenically plastic wrapped food when the date stamp is past. Find the dustbins. Smaller shops may be asked for trimmings to feed to pets, animals - there might be a small charge.

Hotels.

Only the best hotels chuck out stuff when it's going off. Get friendly with the kitchen staff - work there for a week.

Fish shops

Closing time chuck out, on a night with bad business. Crisp batter scraps cost next to nothing.

Parks

Limited range of edibles (see previous section) try acorns or beechmast. Also fishing (see hunting section).

Milk

Milk that has gone sour may be used to make cream cheese (see cooking section).

Blood

Blood donors get free tea and biscuits (and a certificate). In the U.S. they pay you for blood, as they do in many other countries.

Pigeons

Pigeons in large towns are said to be poisonous. I shouldn't imagine sparrows taste too good either! Small non-industrial town birds should be O.K.

Wild Food

Those who think "wild food" is only for country dwellers, are quite wrong. Wild food is available in any park. There is nowhere in Britain where wild food is not available. Food is available wherever plants grow.

Dogmeat ?

Dogmeat is popular in Borneo, New Guinea, E. Asia and Central W. Africa.

Out

If you're really down, begging will easily produce a living, esp. in rich towns.

TOWNS

to survive during lulls in the
natural rhythms of provision.

Bottling Fruit
Particularly useful in preserving fruit that has only a
short season.

The bottling can only be successfully done with proper
vacuum sealing bottles and with
the best, clean, fresh fruit.
The fruit is packed into the
sterilised bottles with sugar,
syrup, golden syrup or honey,
which helps to keep the flavour
good. Water may be used in-
stead of syrup, but the fruit
will have to be sweetened and
reheated before use. The jars
are then closed tight and un-
screwed a quarter turn, heated,
submerged in water, to the
required temperature slowly
(take at least 1 hour.)

Apples, blackberries, gooseberries, loganberries, raspberries, rhubard and strawberries need a temperature of
165°F for ten minutes by this
method. Apricots, cherries,
currants, damsons, citrus
fruits, peaches, plums and
whortleberries require 180°F
for 15 minutes. (Elderberries,
figs and bananas are not very
suitable for bottling.)

After cooling for 24 hours, test
the seal by holding the jar off
the ground slightly by its un-
clipped lid. Time and care must
be taken in bottling. The instructions in your cook book
must be followed exactly or the
bottling will not be successful.

Canning Fruit
The cans and canning machine will
be of a proprietary brand and the
makers' instructions should be
closely followed.
The procedure is similar to that
for bottling. Good fruit and
syrup are put in cans which are
then sealed and put in water
which is brought to the boil.
Apples, apricots, blackberries,
damsons, gooseberries, loganberries, plums, raspberries,
redcurrants, rhubarb, strawberries
are boiled for between 10 and 20
minutes, depending on how long
the water took to boil. Black-
currants, cherries, pears, under-
ripe plums are boiled for 15-20
minutes depending on how quickly
the water boiled.

Bottling Vegetables
Vegetables are much more difficult than fruit to bottle.
In no circumstances, should
bottling or canning of vegetables be done by heating in
boiling water. A higher temperature is needed to kill
bacteria which in the absence
of fruit acids survive boiling.
A pressure cooker is necessary
with a reliable pressure gauge
so that 10 lbs. per sq. inch may
be maintained.
Most vegetables may be bottled
but as the process is rather
long it is usual to preserve
specials, such as asparagus,
peas. As with fruit, it is
essential that they are in good
condition, clean. Hot brine is
used as a covering liquid (1oz.
of salt per quart of water.)
Vegetables are scalded for a
few minutes in boiling water
before being packed.
Celery and asparagus need 10p.s.i.
for 30 minutes, beans, beetroot,
carrots, mushrooms need 35 mins
and peas, new potatoes and mixed
vegetables need 40 mins.
Otherwise the process and testing
is similar to that of bottling
fruit.

Note: the times given above are
for one pint jars, times should
be increased by 5 mins. for two
pint jars.

Canning Vegetables
A pressure cooker is again needed.
Special sulphur resisting cans
are needed also for vegetables.
Before the prepared vegetables
are sealed into the cans, they
are simmered in a pan of water
for about 5 mins. to prevent un-
due strain on the seams when the
sealed cans are in the pressure
cooker. Cans stop at 10 p.s.i.
for 5 mins. less approximately than
bottled vegetables (see above.)
Cans may be cooled quickly in
cold water, but as with bottling,
the pressure in the cooker should
be allowed to fall gradually.

DRYING

Apples, pears, grapes, plums, peas, beans, onions, mushrooms and all herbs may be dried. A drying cupboard with plenty of space and ventilation is needed, with a air temperature of between 120°-150°F which is about the temperature of the average airing cupboard. Apples, pears - slice into rings $\frac{1}{4}$" thick, then submerge in salt water for 5 minutes or so. This will ensure they keep their colour. You can then spread them on trays, thread twine through them, or put them on sticks; anyhow keep them separate.

Peas and Beans - shell and tie in a muslin bag. Put into boiling water, leave for 5 minutes, then plunge into cold water. Dry gradually in a thin layer. Grapes and plums - dry whole or halved. Mushroom and onions - string up (cut onion into rings first) When dry, store in tins or boxes in dry, dark place.

Drying of Meat
Jerky. There is nothing complicated about making jerky. Cut lean, red meat into strips about $\frac{1}{2}$" thick. Hang in the sun, attic or other place where they will dry. At the same time they'll become hard, dry, black and both nourishing and tasty. The strips may first be soaked in brine or sea water. Protect from flies.

For keeping fish. Clean, split into two fillets joined at the tail, smoke over a smouldering fire of green wood such as alder. The fish must be protected from dampness for several days, until dehydrated.

Jams, curds and syrups
The only equipment needed is a large enamel pan and a wooden spoon. Do not make more than 5lbs. of jam from 3lbs. of sugar or the jam will not store well. Cherries, pears, marrow and sweet oranges or grapefruit will need the addition of acid in the form of lemon, redcurrant or gooseberry juice, citric or tartaric acid or commercial pectin before they will set well. Jam recipes are common in many general cookbooks.

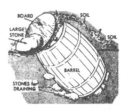

A BARREL ROOT CELLAR can store all or most garden produce in a fresh state over the winter. A strong, well-made barrel should be used and cleaned carefully before being set in trench.

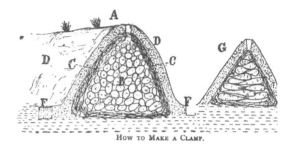

HOW TO MAKE A CLAMP.

Curds. Usually made from oranges or lemons with the addition of margarine, sugar and eggs. Melt 4oz. margarine and mix with grated rind and juice of orange or lemon. Remove from heat, and add beaten eggs (2). Then cook until mixture thickens; after two minutes, remove and jar.

Syrups - made by cooking the fruit very slowly, then drawing off the juice through muslin. The juice is put in bottles which are then simmered in water for 20 minutes. They are then sealed, cooled. Seal checked.

Pickles, Chutneys and Sauces are mainly based on spiced vinegar as the preservative. It is important before pickling vegetables, to put them in a strong brine and leave them to stand. As with jam, it is advisable to use only stainless or enamel lined pans. Chutneys - use apple, marrow, plum and tomato. Pickles use beetroot, blackberries, cucumber, mixed veg, onions, peas, red cabbage, walnuts. Sauces (which are basically sieved chutneys) are made from mint, mushroom, plum or tomato. Follow cookbook recipes.

Salting. A good method of storing beans is in jars between layers of salt. Use dry beans. The salt draws the water from the beans forming brine.

PRESERVING2.

SYNTHESIS

Convenience Foods.

Factory processing of food could make more efficient use of foods, by utilising parts that might be thrown away in the home. What more commonly happens, is that the user loses control of what goes into and what comes out of the food he eats. In exchange for this loss of control, he gains the ubiquitous "time and convenience".

PROTEIN FROM GREENERY,

the function of meat animals can be seen as concentrating protein for the human diet. However, the green leaf plant is a more efficient producer of protein, and recently methods of utilising this protein directly have been developed.

Home Method of Synthesing Protein of green Leaf of Many Kinds.

Almost any kind of non-poisonous greenery may be used. The leaves are first pulped in a home pulper; often known as "the mincer". The juices are collected and the dry material washed through twice with a small amount of water. The remaining juice solutions are then heated to $70-80^{\circ}$c. The leaf protein coagulates at this temperature, and can be separated with a filter process. This can be used directly as food, frozen or dried and ground and kept indefinitely. The small amounts made by a friend of mine Peter Berry, tasted so strongly and strangely, that they were, in their crude state, rather unpalatable to me. However other people were apparently not put off, and the taste is not so evident when the protein is dried and mixed with other foods.

Conclusion:

Ease of manufacture and nutritional value - not in doubt. Palatability needs more work, some doubt at present.

Soya bean or ground nut protein extracts may be "spun" into filament which may be made up into various textures to simulate meats.

SYNTHESIS

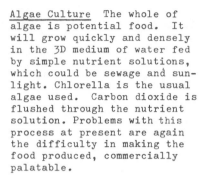

Phenakistoscope.

Algae Culture

The whole of algae is potential food. It will grow quickly and densely in the 3D medium of water fed by simple nutrient solutions, which could be sewage and sunlight. Chlorella is the usual algae used. Carbon dioxide is flushed through the nutrient solution. Problems with this process at present are again the difficulty in making the food produced, commercially palatable.

Yeast is another substance with a fast, dense reproduction rate without light, and a high protein yield. It needs sugar, but this is often a cheap energy source, and ammonium salts. The sulphite residue from paper making is also a possible nutritional base for yeast growth. A particular strain of yeast has been developed that will feed on crude petroleum to produce animal food!

All-Cereal diets may be now made more complete by the addition of the synthesised amino acid Lysine + others depending on the cereal. However, the synthesis of amino acids has been overtaken to some extent, by the plant genetic developments of cereals with a better balance of protein components.

PANTHESIS

In 1950, S.L. Miller passed an electric discharge through a mixture of the gases, methane, hydrogen, water vapour and amonia and found that amino acids were produced. Subsequent experiments by S.W. Fox, at University of Florida found that the 14 amino acids produced were those present in protein, and by further processing, a substance remarkably similar to protein called proteinoid was produced. As a method of synthesising carbohydrate from basic chemicals has been known for about 100 years and the synthesis of vitamins is commercially developed already, it is possible to imagine a totally synthetic life nutrient in the near future. And of course, you are what you eat. Incidentally, fat was produced synthetically in Germany in 1940. The only thing missing is "natural" flavours and aromas - well, these are being investigated at present by gas-liquid chromatography and so within a few years you might not be able to tell quite where your food comes from.

COOKING

Once a popular art, now becoming increasingly a technical skill in the factory,
where much of our super-
market food is cooked up. If
you are going to live on gathered, home grown, scavenged
and cheap bought foods, you need
to redevelop the cooking skills.

Some people say cooking makes
food more digestable and brings
out flavours and aromas, which
are subtle indications of the
nutritive value of the food,
whilst others maintain that cooking does nothing but ruin the
goodness of food: fresh and raw.
There's something to be said
for both views. A few vitamins
do seem to be broken down by
long heating, so it is best to
cook vegetables for the shortest
time possible. Some nutrients
are water soluable, so it is best
to use and lose the minimum of
water. The way to achieve this
is with a pressure cooker. On
cooking potatoes, the tightly
wound structure of natural starch
is broken down and made easier to
digest. There is a similar case
for cooking meats, and many other
hard foods. However, our intestine may like the exercise of
having difficult things to digest
now and again. Who knows? The
only way you can find out, is to
ask your own gut.

BIRCHER MUESLI (original)

1 tblsp. soaked oatmeal for
12 hrs. in 3 tblsp. of water.
1 tbsp. lemon juice
1 tbsp. condensed milk or
top of the milk
1 large apple
1 tbsp. grated hazlenuts &
almonds, cashew or walnuts.
1 teasp. wheat germ

SOUR CREAM & COTTAGE CHEESE

Sour cream is a by-product
obtained from making curd or
cottage cheese from creamy
milk at home. It is a valuable addition for flavour and
nutritional value to all vegetable dishes. 2 pints of un-
pasturised milk produces $\frac{1}{4}$lb.
of curd.
Method:
1. Pour milk into basin, cover
and stand in warm place.
2. Allow to get sour and firm
(2-3 days)
3. Skim off cream and set aside
for cooking.
4. Stand skimmed milk in warmer
place and allow liquid whey to
separate.
5. When whey separates, hang up
to drip in a muslin bag.
Note: to speed up this process,
a spoonful of sour milk from a
previous souring may be added.

YOGHURT: is best made with bulk
bought powdered milk. Use a
clean glass or enamel container.
Half fill with hot water, stir in
powdered milk (1lb. makes 8 pts.)
Then bring the heat up to as hot
as you can bear on your wrist
with boiling water. Add cheap
chainstore bought yoghurt (one
tablespoonful per pint of milk)
and cover or cap. Insulate the
container with a sleeping bag or
newspapers, and leave in a warm
place overnight, or at least
7 hours.

RAW SALAD DRESSING

Ingredients: 2 tbsp. of olive,
nut or any good vegetable oil.
1 tbsp. fresh lemon juice.
Chopped up parsley & chives
or any fresh or dried green
herbs. Some grated onion or
a soupçon of garlic. Arrange
the vegetables like a flower
bed, keeping vegetables separate and taking advantage of
their natural colours. Add
dressing immediately to each
with a teaspoon.
Note: Vegetables should be
picked and prepared as near
to serving as possible. Wash
each thoroughly and separately,
scrubbing roots, after soaking
in a weak salt solution for
$\frac{1}{2}$ hours.

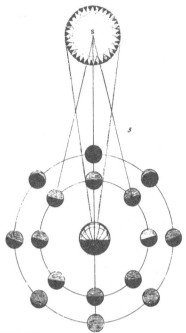

SPROUTS

Fill a glass far about 1/8th full
of beans or peas or wheat. Add
twice the volume of water & allow
to stand 4 hrs. or longer depending on the hardness of the seed,
then keep at 60°-80°F.

Sprouts are ready when the
length of the root is about
4 times that of the pod. May
be exposed to sunlight in the
last 30 minutes, which increases vitamin content.

The seeds must be rinsed in
warm water 3 times daily.
They will take 4-8 days,
depending on the seed.

HOME METHOD FOR SEMI-HARD CHEESE

5 pints fresh milk are put into
a jug and left in a warm place
until solid. Warm this solid
gently in a saucepan until the
curd separates from the whey.
Line a bowl with muslin cloth
and then pour the liquid into
this. The curds and whey are
then suspended in the muslin
above the bowl and left to
drip for 24 hours. The curd
so obtained is then mixed with
salt and beaten well. It is
then put in fresh muslin, and
an approximate 3lb. weight is
left on top for 3 days, changing the muslin every day. The
cheese is then hung in a clean
muslin bag and will keep for
several weeks if stored cool,
and will become stronger as
it is left.

PIGEON, CASSEROLE

After plucking & cleaning them
out, halve 2 pigeons, roll them
in flour and brown them in oil
or fat in a casserole. Remove
pigeons when brown, and add a
little flour to the casserole,
stirring well. Add a glass of
warm water or red wine, and then
1lb. of peas, a few small onions,
seasoning and lastly the pigeons.
Cover the casserole & cook in
oven until tender. Other small
game such as rabbits & squirrel
can be cooked in a similar fash-
ion. Cut into thin strips,
roll in flour etc.

FROGS LEGS similar to chicken.

Both front & back legs are edible. The smaller the frog,
the more tender and sweet they
are. Strip off skin like a
glove, and grill or fry gently.

SIMPLE CAMP BREAD

If you don't have a mixing surface or bowl when making bread,
it may be made in the flour
sack. Make a hollow in the
flour, then add salt & baking
powder, then, whilst mixing
with one hand, add water with
the other, until the resulting
dough has picked up sufficient
flour. Small buns, or french
loaf type twist rolls may be
made from this mixture over an
open fire. Eat them as soon
as they are done for maximum
enjoyment

FRUMITY

Ears of corn, rubbed and shaken
until seed is free from husks
and put in a big store jar with
enough milk to cover. The jar
is stood on the edge of a smouldering peat fire (ideal) until
the next day. It is then eaten
hot for breakfast with more
milk and honey.

ACORN BREAD

Mix 4 cups of acorn flour with
3 tbsp. butter, 2/3rds. cup of
sugar. 3 teasp. baking powder,
1/3rd. teasp. salt, 2 eggs and
2 cups of milk. Beat well.
Bake at 350° for 20 mins.

WILD FLOWER CONSERVE

Ingredients - cowslip, elecampane
flower and root, honeysuckle &
primrose. Pound flowers to a
pulp in a pestle & mortar. Add equal amounts
of sugar and mix well together.

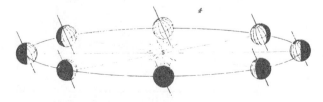

RECIPES

EXCRETA, wherever deposited, immediately start
to decompose and are ultimately converted to an
inodorous, inoffensive and stable product. Proteins
and urea are reduced to simpler and more stable
forms producing such gasses as methane, carbon
dioxide, ammonia and nitrogen, which are
released into the atmosphere (or in a compost
system may be collected and used as fuel.) The
bacterial action of decomposition is either aerobic,
in the presence of air, or anaerobic, or a process
which involves both stages. The decomposition
takes from several months up to nearly a year
under average conditions in a pit privy. The
decomposition process is unfavourable to the
survival of pathogenic organisms. The final
products contain valuable soil nutrients and may
be used as fertilizer ———————————

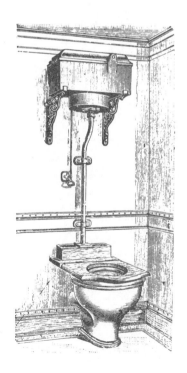

The experts are unanimously agreed
as to the ideal posture for defaecation.
Squatting in every way decreases
unnecessary strain and encourages
the complete expulsion of the faecal
mass. The knees being at least above
the seat level.
So here we have the common or
garden W.C. It gives you haemorrhoids,
wastes untold amounts of pure water
in flushing and wastes good fertilizer
from your own body.
Down with the cistern!

WASTE?

Quantities of Human Faeces

For European countries approx. 5.3oz. faeces per day. In N. America a figure for pit privy design is based on 1.5cu.ft. per person per year where water may leak away and a figure of 19.5 cu.ft. for a water tight privy. However, available data being meagre, a total daily per person excreta weight of 2.2lb, (wet) should be used.

Soil and Ground water pollution

Horizontal travel of bacteria through the soil from a privy is usually less than 3 ft. and downward travel less than 10ft. in pits open to heavy rains, and 2 ft. in normally porous soils. However, if underground water intersects this region, bacterial travel may be as much as 100ft, (though more usually 36ft) in the direction of the aquifer flow, with a maximum width of 6ft. Bacteria will not travel upstream against the flow.
Chemical pollution in aquifer is much greater than bacteria, and may travel 300ft or more with a maximum width of 30ft. again only downstream. Of course it is important that water drawing points are not located within these areas.

Fly breeding in Excreta

Many houseflies will breed on human excrement and later carry harmful organisms to human food. In latrine design, flies can be avoided by use of the fact that flies are attracted by light, and shun darkness, i.e. the pit should be closed when not in use. Disinfectants are of little use in pit latrines, as they are quickly neutralised by the organic matter. They also interfere with bacterial decomposition.
Note: a 1" layer of 10% Borax Solution in a latrine is an effective control to fly breeding.

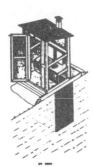

The Pit Privy

Usually a round or square pond 3'-4' wide, depth will vary from 6'-16' depending on local conditions. It is usually about 8'.

Life of a Pit

It is recommended that pits should be designed for a life of at least 4 years. With suitable soil conditions, this may be increased anything up to 10-15 years.
When the level of excreta comes within 20" of the ground surface, the pit should be closed with earth. A new pit should be built near the old one, and the super structure moved over it. The faeces in the old pit are left to decompose for 9-12 months, after which it may be dug out and used as fertiliser. The cleanest pit may then be re-used. Disinfectants should not be added. A cupful of kerosene each week in the pit will prevent mosquitoes breeding.

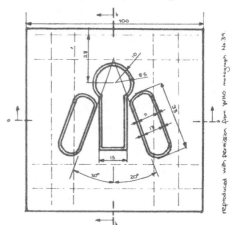

reproduced with permission from WHO monograph № 39

Lining of the Pit

It is often necessary to line a pit to prevent the sides from caving in especially in unstable soils. Even in stable soils, it is desirable to line the top 24". Bricks, stones, concrete blocks, adobe, timber, split cane may be used. Open joints being formed around walls are stronger than square. The floor should fit tightly onto the base which may be of soil cement or clay.
Note: to reduce condensation on the outside of the cover, an insect proof vent should be fitted.

THE AQUA PRIVY

The aqua privy is a water filled tank into which there is
a drip pipe. Anaerobic decomposition of the faeces reduces
it to a digested sludge which
must be removed at intervals.
Tanks may be made from whatever is locally available, but
must be water-tight. Concrete
tanks are usually rectangular
because of the shuttering. A
round tank may be made from a
plain concrete sewer pipe with
the end sealed with concrete.
One cubic meter (35cu.ft) tank
for a family will allow sludge
to be removed once every 6 yrs.

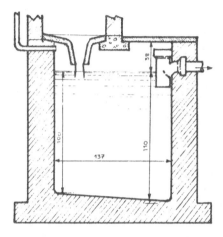

For each litre of water added
to the tank, a corresponding
amount of sewage water must be
disposed of as effluent.
Usually by seepage pits or
sub-surface irrigation.

A properly operated aqua privy
is a clean and odourless inst-
alation which may be safely
placed close to a dwelling.
Sludge from such a privy
should be buried in trenches 16"
deep.
Note: A privy may be seeded
with the right bacteria with
digested sludge bailed from
another privy though this is
not necessary, the tank seeding
itself within 6-8 weeks. Should
the privy be in use daily, about
5-8 gallons of water should be
flushed down.

Note: it has been found that
contaminated material in liquid
suspension can remain viable
for as long as six months. i.e.
a much longer time in anaerobic
conditions than in aerobic conditions.

Water Seal Latrine or pan flush
unit-

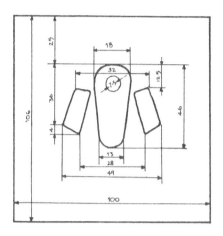

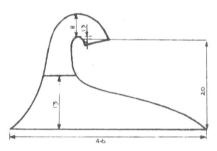

One to three quarts of water are
sufficient to flush such a unit
which may be fitted over a pit
or aqua pit system. This seal
may be made from concrete around
a clay form or in two halves,
which are carefully joined together.

The pour flush unit can be installed within a house if a re-
ceiving pit can be built nearby
outside. The connecting pipe in
such a system should be 4-6"
diameter and built at a steep
slope (not less than 5°.)

Other advantages of a water
sealed pour flush are complete
sealing against odour and insects, less chance of things
falling into the pit.
Disadvantage: needs a continuous supply of water in the
privy.

Earth Closet

In this system, a mechanical device releases dry earth, saw dust or ash to cover the excreta which is caught in a bucket. Collection needs to be made daily and immediately replaced with a second disinfected bucket.

1. Contents are disposed of into a pit to decompose aerobically or anaerobically (aqua pit.)
2. Into trenches 24" deep. 12" excrement, 18" soil cover.
3. Into sewer.

This system, although theoretically workable rarely works well in practice as it is open to abuse and needs regular and reliable servicing. It can only be recommended as a collector of "night soil."

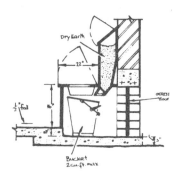

Trench Latrine.

With particular relevance to camping and short stays in areas of low population. The trench is usually about 24" deep and between 3' and 10' long

This method relies on excreta being quickly digested by the aerobic saprophylic bacteria, numerous and active in the upper part of the soil, which will reduce the excreta within 8 weeks. It is good practice to cover the filled trench for the digestion period (2 months) with an iron sheet (against animals, rain run-off, soil pollution with worm larvae.)

Compost Privy

By this method, a pit privy is managed to provide useful fertiliser for the land, without the necessity of handling raw excreta. Before the floor slab of the pit is laid, the bottom 20" of the pit is filled with grass cuttings, fire leaves, cooking garbage, paper or any other biodegradable rubbish. In addition to human excrement, throw the daily garbage into the pit, along with cow, horse, sheep, chicken and pig manure as well as urine soaked earth and straw (see composting page About once a week add some textured plant waste to the pit. When the contents reach a level 20" below the ground level, a new pit is dug at least 6' away and the super structure and slab moved over it. The first pit is covered with a layer of fine plant material then with well tamped earth. When the second pit is filled, it will be time to empty the first pit and distribute or store it as necessary.

The cycle for a 35.cu.ft. pit if about 1/5th of the fill is excreta would be about 9-10 months for a family of five. The ideal arrangement is the double vault privy.

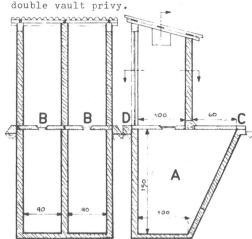

Each part is used alternately. Good supervision is essential for the proper workings of the compost privy.

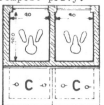

EARTH.

CHEMICAL TOILETS

These may either be simple buckets containing chemical fluid or a tank attached to a toilet seat. The deodorised chemical fluid used which breaks up the fecal matter, may be caustic soda. For a tank with a capacity of 100 gallons, a charge of 25lbs. of caustic soda is dissolved in 11 gallons of water. The bucket type, commonly used in caravans, often use a proprietary fluid such as "Elsan Blue" or "Racason", which is safe and convenient, but rather expensive.

Tank models are often supplied with an agitator to break up solid matter. After several months of operation, the spent liquified excrement and chemical is drained off to a suitably located cess pool or tank, from which the remnant may be used as manure.

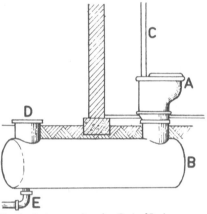

Bucket type chemical toilets must be emptied more frequently, and if you use a suitable chemical such as Elsan Blue, the contents may be poured onto the garden as manure (providing the last charge has been given time to liquify.)

FOLDING TOILET

A lightweight portable toilet with a regular size plastic seat and tubular alloy frame, providing standard toilet height of 17", weight 4 lbs. Folded size 20" x 14" x 1½". Complete with 6 strong white polythene bags with draw strings. Toilet size folded 16" x 11".

Price **£2.50** (£2.10.0.)

Permanent installation

To make a permanent domestic installation, you need only a small pit – 3′ x 3′ x 3′ is sufficient – and almost fill it with hard core. Cover with a sheet of heavy duty polythene and replace earth to ground level. This acts as a permanent soakaway, so that you have a sanitation system as hygienic

Perdisan 'CADET'

Ideal for touring, caravans, buses, etc. Comes with floor-holding fixtures. Suitable for portable or for permanent installation. Completely watertight, a boon when travelling.

Perdisan – the complete convenience

The seat and seat lid, which are easily detachable are made in virtually unbreakable high-quality Abstrene and are hinged to the main container.

The Rally model is fitted with an anti-spill lid made from polypropylene, light, strong and easy to keep clean, with six polypropylene integral clips for locking on to the container.

The container is in blue polypropylene and is fitted with a stainless steel carrying handle.

The Rally model is fitted with quick release polypropylene floor fixtures.

ELSAN

DIMENSIONS		
14¾" (37·4 cm)	:	Height
14¼" (36·2 cm)	:	Width
17¼" (43·7 cm)	:	Depth
4 gallons (18·2 litres)	:	Capacity
(Standard Model) 5¾ lb. (2·60 kgs)	:	Weight
(Rally Model) 6¾ lb. (3·06 kgs)		

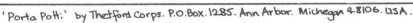

'Porta Potti.' by Thetford Corps. P.O.Box. 1285. Ann Arbor. Michegan 48106. USA.

CHEMICAL

Water carried disposal

Where water is in plentiful
supply, it is certainly most
hygenic when this is conn-
ected to a sewage system.
Otherwise the excess dilution
causes problems. Various
methods of disposal are used.
1. Disposal by dilution -
possible when sea, lake or a
large river is nearby. But to
be avoided wherever possible.
2. The Cesspool. A covered pit
that receives raw sewage. It
may be of the water-tight or of
the leaching type, depending on
soil and population density.
Water tight pools are designed
for 15 gallons per person per
month. A leaching cesspool
(i.e. liquid seep off) must not
be downhill from a well and/or
at least 50ft. away - where
chemical pollution is possible
150ft.

The seepage pit

Receives effluent from aqua
privies, cess pools and septic
tanks and allows it to percolate
into the ground. Also used for
other household wastes.

Syphon discharge

Delivers sewage at intervals
and with more force reduces
clogging of ground or filters.
Expense usually limits use of
this item to larger systems.

Note: It is worth consulting
a sanitary engineer if medium
size sewaging is foreseen. e.g.
for a school or a large commune.
Don't forget this system won't
work if you put disinfectants
etc. or poisons that kill bacteria into it!

Septic Tank

The most hygenic small water
carried system. It consists
of a small settling tank into
which the raw sewage is lead.
In this , a primary treatment
takes place under anaerobic
decomposition for one, two or
three days. The heavier solids
stay in the tank and reduce
considerably in volume. The
effluent from these tanks goes
on to a secondary treatment with
oxidation of organic matter by
aerobic bacteria., in sub-surface
irrigation or on filter beds.
Sub-surface irrigation is only
acceptable where the conditions
are right i.e. light sandy soil.
Where ground water is close to
the surface, it may not be possible to dispose of the effluent
through sub-surface irrigation
as the pores of the soil above
the water table are clogged by
water held by capilliary action.
The pipes shouldn't be laid closer
than 3' to the ground water level.

Tank size.

consider:
(a) average daily flow of sewage.
(b) retention period, usually
    24 hours.
(c) adequate sludge storage for
    desludging 2-3 years.

for 6 people, this is 600 gallons
3' x7' x5' .

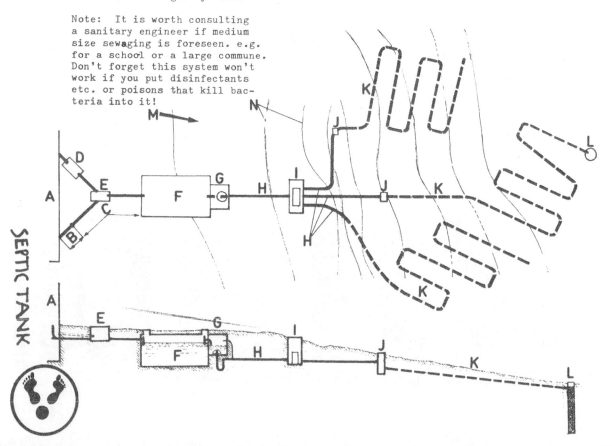

SEPTIC TANK

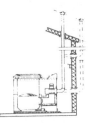

D4 Electric toilet
Partille E. C. Verken, Aktiebolag,
Partille-Sweden.

The fan and heater element
that frys your excrement, only
needs connecting to a vent pipe
and a 240v supply. After use
the lid closes and heat comes
on at the press of a button.
Combustion time varies between
10 and 30 minutes, but the
closet can be used several times
during this period. There is
also the added feature of red
and green control lamps for the
fan and heater element. Hate
to think what would happen if
this one got out of control!

In another electricity pan a
low voltage electric current
passes between electrodes
emersed in the sewage releas-
ing chlorine, oxygen and other
elements which sterilise and
oxidise the organic content.

Nitrogenous substances discharge
in sewage effluent contains
about 1/3rd of the country's
needs in nitrogenous fertilisers.
Biological treatment of water
is usually costly because of the
necessity for oxygen to be supplied to the bacteria. However,
a cheap method of providing this
oxygen without costly maintenance
is.......Algae. As a product of
photosynthesis Algae produce oxygen and absorb nitrogen, phos-
phorous and potash. The Algae
are harvested as food, fodder
or manure.

"Modern" Version of the Compost Privy.

Ken Kern, in his book "Owner
Built Home" suggests that a
circular tower should be built.
On top of this tower is a solar
heat collector that heats the
water in an adjacent tank.
This water supplies a shower.
The shower compartment has a
pour flush unit in the floor
and under this floor are the
composting chambers. The
shower hose is also used to
flush the toilet which is a
simple squatting plate. There
are chutes for other biodegradable wastes to enter the composting chambers and a sealed
door by which the mature compost
might be removed. Add a wind
generating propellor to the top
of this   to pump up water(and
heat the water when the sun isn't
out) & a water collection pipe
from the adjacent house roof and
this would be an ecologically sound
independent set up.

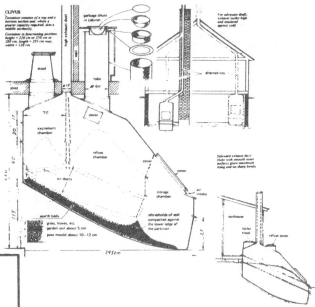

This Swedish composting system
is a very hygenic and elegant
design of glass reinforced poly-
ester construction. It comes as a
single unit ready for operation.
Cost including importing charges
is around £250-300. See bibliography
eight.
This system, which could be very
cheap   if home-made, conserves
water, disposes of refuse and
produces organic compost. With
some modification it could collect
the gases of decomposition for
power uses.

MISCELLANEOUS

WASTE NOT
WANT NOT
WASTE NOT
NEED KNOT

provision for dustbins off street. Communal bins have separate compartments for different materials

Waste separated at source for recycling.

lorry engine works on gases from decomposing waste inside. economical and non-polluting

community volunteer works on the bins one day per year

Camping wet and dry waste pits

Two pits about 2ft x 1ft deep. The bottom of the wet pit is covered with grass and all greasy and wet refuse is put in here. The grass, which is burnt and replaced each day, stops the ground getting clogged up. The dry pit holds all other rubbish that cannot be burnt. Burning tin cans removes the laquer and tinning, so that they will rust quicker. Some earth should be sprinkled over the contents of this pit every evening.

When leaving a wet pit or food garbage pit shallower than 2ft. pour some paraffin on the ground after you have filled the pit, so as to deter animals from digging it up.

Hove Corporation collect their paper separately in a trailer and recycle it. This is a good thing. Get your Council onto it. If they had another trailer they could recycle metals as well. Investigate where your waste goes see that it doesn't come to no good.

BRENCO NO LITTER PLEASE

90 · FAIRLY GOOD   100 · MARKSMAN

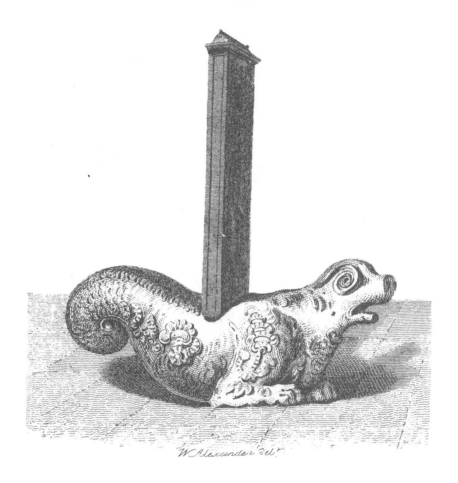

W. Alexander Del.

BIBLIOGRAPHY

INFO AREA 1   INTRODUCTION GENERAL

ADAM M. JAMES LT.COL.   A Traveller's Guide to Health   Sphere 1966
Agricultural Atlas of England & Wales   Faber & Faber 1964
ANDERSON, M.S.   Geography of Living Things   E.U.P. 1951
BOYD ORR, Sir John.   Food & The People   Pilot Press 1943
BROTHINELI, Don & Patricia.   Food in Antiquity   Thames & Hudson
CIVIL DEFENCE HANDBOOK No.8 Basic Feeding No.7 Rescue Manual
FORESTRY COMMISSION.   Grants for woodland owners (free post free pamphlet.)
GARNER J.F.   The Law of Allotments   Shaw
HEATH S.P. ed.   The future of Hill Farming   Reading University Agric.Club. 1969
KROPOTKIN.   Farms, Factories & Workshops
HOWARD Sir Albert.   An Agricultural Testament   Oxford 1940
∗ MAYCOCK S.A. & MAYHURST J. editors.   The Small Holder Encyclopedia   Pearson 1950
MAYCOCK S.A.   Living from the Land   Pearson 1947
∗ MOTHER EARTH NEWS P.O. Box 38, Madison, Ohio 44057 U.S.A.
              $6 six issues. One years subscription. $1-$1.25 per issue
ORDISH, George.   The Living House   Rupert Hart Davis . 1959

Info Area 1.

Oxford Book of Food Plants

PHILBRICK H. & GREGG R.B.   Companion Plants

PIKE, Magnus.   Food and Society   Murray 1968
                Man and Food   Wiedenfeld Nicholson.   1970

PIRIE, N.W.   Food Resources Conventional & Novel   Pelican 1969

SOIL ASSOCIATION.   Man and His Environment New Bells Farm,   1966
                    Haughly, Stowmarket, Suffolk.

The Nature Conservancy Handbook (SBN 11 880301 8)   H.M.S.O.1968

THOMPSON Alan.   Your Smallholding   Penguin 1947

WESTON W.J.   Law and the Countryman

WOODHEAD The Study of Plants   Oxford (pre war?)

KAYSINGS, B.   First-time Farmers Guide   Straight Arrow 1971

INFO AREA 2 NUTRITION

BALFOUR Michael edit.   Health Food Guide   Garnstone 1970

BEHSERA Michael A   Zen Macrobiotic Cooking   Albyn 1969

DEPT. OF HEALTH & SOCIAL SECURITY.   Recommended Intake of
                        Nutrients for U.K.   H.M.S.O.

DRUMMOND J.C. & WILPRAHAM, Anne. The Englishmans Food – 5 centuries of
                        English Diet   J. Cape 1957

Food Values at a Glance   The Food Education Soc. 160 Picadilly, London W.1

HARTLEY, Dorothy.   Food in England   Macdonald 1954

HARACH Al & RENDLE T. ed.   The Nations Food

✳MIN. OF AGRICULTURE.   Manual of Nutrition   H.M.S.O. 1961

OSHOWA, George.   The Macrobiotic Guidebook for Living. Oshowa Foundation 1967

PIKE, Magnus.   Man and Food   World Univ. Library 1971

STILES W.   Trace Elements in Plants & Animals   Cambridge 1946

YOGI VITHALDAS & SUSAN ROBERTS.   The Yogi Cookbook   Crown 1968

✳LAPPE, F.M.   Diet for a Small Planet   Ballantine 1971

LONGGOOD, W.   The Poisons in Your Food   Pyramid Books 1971

KINGSBURY. J.M.   Deadly Harvest   George Allen & Unwin 1967

INFO AREA 3 AIR

AGRICULTURAL RESEARCH COUNCIL.   The Effects of Air Pollutants on Plants
                        and the Soil.   H.M.S.O. 30p 1967

Air pollution. Monograph series No.46 £2.   W.H.O.1961

Atmospheric Pollutants. Technical Report series 271 9p.   W.H.O.1963

CHANDLER, T.C.   The Air Around Us   Aldous 1967

C.O.I. for Dept. of Employment and Productivity. Carbon Monoxide
        Poisoning: Causes & Prevention. Health & Safety At Work No. 29 17½p.
                                                          H.M.S.O.

Epidemiology of Air Pollution Public Health Paper 15.   W.H.O. 1961

GARNER. J.F.   Clean Air – Law & Practice   Shaw

MORRIS, Margaret.   Breathing Exercises   Margaret Morris London 1935

NADER. Vanishing Air S0.95   Exposito 1970

The Breathers Guide to Invisible Air Pollution Fact file 1. Ecology
                Information Group. 20 Crystal Way, Berkely. CA. USA.

BIBLIOGRAPHY TWO

INFO AREA 4 WATER

ALLISEBROOK, C. Water Supply. Water Ways No.8 Guthrie Allisebrook & Co.,
Reading.

ALWOOD, R. & LAWARD, T.A. The Cost of Collecting Rainwater for Use in
Isolated Communities. Tec. memo T47. BRACE.

BAREMAN, G.H. A Bibliography of Low-cost Water Technologies.
Intermediate Technology Group £1.   1971

C.O.I. for Min. of Public Building & Works, & Min. of Housing &
Local Government. Water Pollution Control Engineering.   H.M.S.O. 1972
Note: this was compiled by the WATER POLLUTION RESEARCH LAB. Elderway,
London Road, Stevenage, Herts, who will provide a list of publications on
request.

Community Water Supply Tech. report series No. 420 20p.   W.H.O.

DELWYN DAVIES, Fresh Water   Aldous 1967

DUMBLETON, J.E. Wells and Boreholes for Water Supply   1953

European Standards for Drinking Water 40p   W.H.O. 1970

GIBSON, H.P. & SINGER R.D. Small Wells Manual Health Service Office of
War on Hunger, Washington D.C.

GIFFIN, Frank. Water Supply. The Mechanical Age Library   Muller 1965

✳ HARTLEY, Dorothy. Water in England   Macdonald 1964

Health Implications of Water Related Parasite Diseases in Water
Development Areas.   F.A.O. & W.H.O. 1967

Min. of Defence. The Location of Underground Water by Geological &
Geophysical Methods. Military Enginerring Vol. V1 –
Water Supply Suppl. No. 1 April 12th 1945.   H.M.S.O.

Min. of the Environment (Water Resources Board) Report of Desalination
for England and Wales. (SBN 11 780002 3) 20p.   1969

UNDERWOOD, Guy Patterns of the Past   Pitman 1970

VEAL, T.H.P. The Supply of Water.   Chapman & Hall 1950

✳ WAGNER, E.G. & LANOIX, J.N. Water Supply for Rural Areas & Small
Communities. (mono. series No. 42) S6.75.
W.H.O. 1959

MARTIN A. Edward. Dewponds   T. Wierner Laurie 1910

INFO AREA 5 GROWING

BENDERS, Roy. Mushroom Growing for Everyone   Faber 1969

BENTLY Soil-less Gardening for Flat & Home   Blandford 1957

✳ BOFF, Charles How to Grow and Produce your Own Food   Odhams 195?

BROWN, E.T. Make Your Garden Feed You   Literary Press, Glasgow. W.W.11.

EASEY, Ben Practical Organic Gardening   Faber & Faber

FLAVIN, Louis N. Profitable Gardening (Smallholders Guide)   1961

GERICKE, Dr. William F. Complete Guide to Soilless Gardening
(Hydroponics)   Putnam 1941

GREE, Donald Diseases of vegetables   Macmillan

HARVEY JAMES, Irma   Unusual vegetables   Hunt Davies 1956

HILLS, Laurence D. Russian Comfrey   Faber & Faber 1953

HILYER C. Isabel Hydroponics   Pelican Special 1940

HILTON A.C. Rural Science and School Gardening   Batsford 1959

✳ HOLLIS, H.F. Profitable Growing without Soil   E.U.P. 1964

LOCKWOOD, Crosby. Vegetable Growers Guide   Oldham

Feeding the Fifty Million can Britain be self-supporting
in Food?   Hollis & Carter 1955

MAUNSEL, J. E. B. Natural Gardening   Faber 1958

O'BRIEN, Danziel Intensive Gardening   Faber 1956

Pictorial Food Growing   Crowther. W. W. 11

RODALE, J. I. How to Grow Fruit & Veg. by the Organic Method

RODEL, Robert, ed. The Basic Book of Organic Gardening   Ballantine

SAUNBY, T. Soilless Culture   Collingridge 1953

SEIFERT, Alwin. Compost   Faber & Faber 1962

∗ SHOLTO DOUGLAS, J. Hydroponics - The Bengal System 90p. 4th ed. Oxford 1970

                     Beginners Guide to Hydroponics £2.25   Pelham 1972

SIMPSON A. J. Flowers & Vegetables Without Soil
               National Council of Social Service. London.

SINCLAIR RHODE, Eleanor. Uncommon Vegetables   Country Life 1943
                                                         reprinted '46

The Culture of Plants In Sand & Aggregate Jealotts Hill Research Station,
                                                     Bracknell, Berks

TIQUET, E. E. Successful Gardening Without Soil   Pearson 1952

WHITEHEAD. Plain Vegetable Growing   Black 1941

WITHAM- FOGG, H. G. Vegetables All Year Round   Stanley Paul 1966

The Whole Food Finder publ. by Henry Doubleday Association, Bocking,
   Braintree, Essex and The Soil Association, New Bells Farm, Haughley,
   Stowmarket, Suffolk. A directory of shops, farmers, amateur gardeners
   who sell organic food, i.e. grown without artificial fertilisers, pesticides or fungicides.

∗ The Henry Doubleday Association subs. £2. p.a.
   Organic gardening advice free to members, 10/- to non-members. The
   association is non profitmaking engaged in the following research.
   Russian Comfrey (all aspects), The control of pests and diseases
   without chemicals, compost and green manure and the testing of new
   vegetable and fodder crops in Britain and overseas. publ:
                     Fertility Without Fertilisers   3/6 post free.
                     Pest Control Without Poisons   3/6 post free.

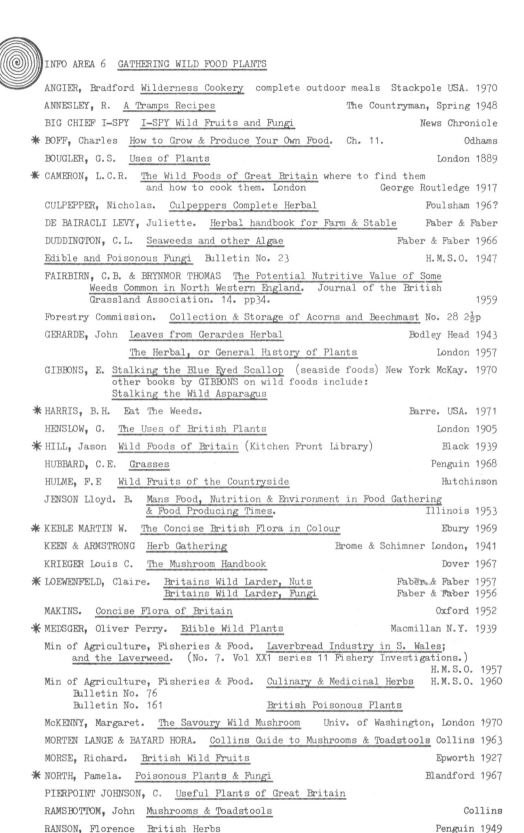

ANGIER, Bradford Wilderness Cookery complete outdoor meals Stackpole USA. 1970

ANNESLEY, R. A Tramps Recipes   The Countryman, Spring 1948

BIG CHIEF I-SPY I-SPY Wild Fruits and Fungi   News Chronicle

✳ BOFF, Charles How to Grow & Produce Your Own Food. Ch. 11.   Odhams

BOUGLER, G.S. Uses of Plants   London 1889

✳ CAMERON, L.C.R. The Wild Foods of Great Britain where to find them
                  and how to cook them. London   George Routledge 1917

CULPEPPER, Nicholas. Culpeppers Complete Herbal   Foulsham 196?

DE BAIRACLI LEVY, Juliette. Herbal handbook for Farm & Stable   Faber & Faber

DUDDINGTON, C.L. Seaweeds and other Algae   Faber & Faber 1966

Edible and Poisonous Fungi Bulletin No. 23   H.M.S.O. 1947

FAIRBIRN, C.B. & BRYNMOR THOMAS The Potential Nutritive Value of Some
              Weeds Common in North Western England. Journal of the British
              Grassland Association. 14. pp34.   1959

Forestry Commission. Collection & Storage of Acorns and Beechmast No. 28 2½p

GERARDE, John Leaves from Gerardes Herbal   Bodley Head 1943

          The Herbal, or General History of Plants   London 1957

GIBBONS, E. Stalking the Blue Eyed Scallop (seaside foods) New York McKay. 1970
          other books by GIBBONS on wild foods include:
          Stalking the Wild Asparagus

✳ HARRIS, B.H. Eat The Weeds.   Barre. USA. 1971

HENSLOW, G. The Uses of British Plants   London 1905

✳ HILL, Jason Wild Foods of Britain (Kitchen Front Library)   Black 1939

HUBBARD, C.E. Grasses   Penguin 1968

HULME, F.E Wild Fruits of the Countryside   Hutchinson

JENSON Lloyd. B. Mans Food, Nutrition & Environment in Food Gathering
              & Food Producing Times.   Illinois 1953

✳ KEBLE MARTIN W. The Concise British Flora in Colour   Ebury 1969

KEEN & ARMSTRONG Herb Gathering   Brome & Schimner London, 1941

KRIEGER Louis C. The Mushroom Handbook   Dover 1967

✳ LOEWENFELD, Claire. Britains Wild Larder, Nuts   Faber & Faber 1957
                      Britains Wild Larder, Fungi   Faber & Faber 1956

MAKINS. Concise Flora of Britain   Oxford 1952

✳ MEDSGER, Oliver Perry. Edible Wild Plants   Macmillan N.Y. 1939

Min of Agriculture, Fisheries & Food. Laverbread Industry in S. Wales;
          and the Laverweed. (No. 7. Vol XX1 series 11 Fishery Investigations.)
                                                    H.M.S.O. 1957
Min of Agriculture, Fisheries & Food. Culinary & Medicinal Herbs H.M.S.O. 1960
      Bulletin No. 76
      Bulletin No. 161   British Poisonous Plants

McKENNY, Margaret. The Savoury Wild Mushroom Univ. of Washington, London 1970

MORTEN LANGE & BAYARD HORA. Collins Guide to Mushrooms & Toadstools Collins 1963

MORSE, Richard. British Wild Fruits   Epworth 1927

✳ NORTH, Pamela. Poisonous Plants & Fungi   Blandford 1967

PIERPOINT JOHNSON, C. Useful Plants of Great Britain

RAMSBOTTOM, John Mushrooms & Toadstools   Collins

RANSON, Florence British Herbs   Penguin 1949

SALISBURY, Sir Edward. Weeds & Aliens   Collins 1961

SANECKI K.N. Wild & Garden Herbs   Collingbridge

SAUNDERS, Charles F. Useful Wild Plants of the U.S. & Canada.
                                  Robert M. McBridg. N.Y. 1920

STURTEVANT, E.L. Notes on Edible Plants   Albany. N.Y. 1919

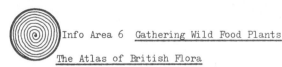

Info Area 6   Gathering Wild Food Plants

The Atlas of British Flora   B.S.B.I. & Nelson 1962

The Epicures Companion   Dent & Sons London 1937

✳ THORNE QUELCH, Mary Herbs for Daily Use   Faber & Faber 1952
                                                        reprinted 1969

    WYNNE, HATEFIELD, Audrey. Pleasures of Wild Plants   Museum 1966
                               How to Enjoy Your Weeds   Muller 1969

✳ ZEITLMAYR. Linus. Wild Mushrooms, an illustrated Handbook   Muller 1968

INFO AREA 7   REARING ANIMALS

BARDACH, J.E., McLARNEY W.O., RYTHER, J. Aquaculture Wiley & Sons N.Y. 1972

BIRTWHISTLE, V. Duck-keeping for Pleasure & Profit   Pearson 1946

BRETT, W. Eggs from Your Garden   Pearson 1940

BROWN, E.T. The 'How to do it' Poultry Book   Pearson 1927

Dept. of Agriculture & Fisheries for Scotland. Fish Farming:
    A Guide to the Design & Construction of net enclosures. Marine
    Research No. 1. 90p   1970

FRANCIS, F. Fish-Culture, a Practical Guide Routledge Warne, Routledge 1865

GEARY, H. Profitable beekeeping   Pearson 1911

HARRISON, N. Survival Piece / Portable Fish Farm
              Arch. Design mag. November 1971

HICKLING C.F. Fish Culture £4.50   Faber 1962-71

LE CREN, E.D. The Application of Science to Inland Fisheries   F.A.O. 1958

Min. of Agriculture, Fisheries & Food. Fisheries notice No.29
              Commerical Trout Culture; Lab. Leaflets No.22 Which Fish
              To Farm; No. 23 Cornish Cray Fish Investigation
              Oyster Cultivation in Britain. A manual of current
              practices. out of print

Min of Environment. Model Byelaws. 11C For the keeping of animals so as
              to be prejudicial to health. reprinted 1968 3½p. H.M.S.O.

✳ MAYCOCK S.A. & HAYHURST J. ed. The Smallholders Encyclopedia   Pearson 1950

New Alchemy Institute Aquaculture/agriculture project
              P.O. Box 432, Woodshole, Massachusetts 02543, USA.

SCHUSTER W.H. et al. Fish Farming & Inland Fishery Management in Rural
              Economy.   F.A.O. 1954

INFO AREA 8   HUNTING ANIMALS

BLANDFORD P.W. Netmaking   Brown Sons & Ferguson, Glasgow. (recent.)

BODENHEIMER, F.S. Insects as Human Food   The Hage 1951

CLARKE, G. The Stone Age Hunters   Thames & Hudson 1967

DUNCAN & THORNE The Complete Wildfowler (ashore & afloat)
                                         Herbert Jenkins. 1950

FORSYTH, W.S. Lobster & Crab Fishing   A & C Black 1946

HODGKIN The Archers Craft   Faber & Faber

HEATH, A. From Creel to Kitchen Fresh water fish & how to eat them   1940

HUNT & METZ. The Flat Bow   Bruce (U.S.A) 1941

LAURENCE WELLS, A. The observers book of Fresh Water Fishes   F. Warne

Info Area 8 Hunting Animals

Min. of Agriculture, Fisheries & Food.
   Fisheries Notices No. 9 Capture of Eels
                       No. 36 The Elementary Practice of Electrical fishing
                              in fresh water

NIALL, A. A Poachers Handbook   Heinemann 1950

SANDYS—WINSCH G. Gun Law   Shaw 1969

Forestry Commission Rabbit Control in Woodlands H.M.S.O. 1965 20p
                     Animals & Birds Booklet No. 14
                     The Grey Squirrel 1962 9p.
                     Animals & Birds Leaflet No. 31
             also Animals & Birds Forest Record No. 66 Blackgame 1968 15p.
                                               No. 76 Polecats 1970 15p
                                               No. 77 Hedgehogs 1970 15p
             also Research & Development Papers (free)
                  No. 32 The Utilisation of Bark by J.R. Aaron 1970
                  No. 61 The Grey Squirrel & His Control, Miss J.J. Row 1967
             available from: Forestry Commission, 25 Savile Row, London W.1.

WALKER, R. Rod Building for Amateurs   Angling Times 1963

MOSS, L How to Build & Repair your own Fishing Rod   Technical Press 1969

BRUCE, Dr. R. Cheaper Tackle   A.C. Black 1960

INFO AREA No. 9 COOKING, PRESERVING, PROCESSING Etc.

CONSUMER CO—OP The Co—op Low—cost Cookbook   Consumer Co—op Berkeley 1965

HEATON, N. compiler. Traditional Recipes of the British Isles   Faber 1951

HUNTER, B.T.A. The Natural Foods Cookbook   Consumer Co—op Berkeley 1965

LUTES, D. The Country Kitchen   Bell 1938

Min of Agriculture, Fisheries & Food.
            Edible & Poisonous Fungi Bulletin No, 23   H.M.S.O. 1947
            ABC of Preserving   "   1949
            Culinary & Medicinal Herbs Bulletin No. 76   "   1960

YOGI VITHALDAS & SUSAN ROBERTS The Yogi Cookbook   Crown 1968

McNEIL, F.M. The Scots Kitchen   London 1959

INFO AREA 10 WASTE NOT

BLAKE, E.H. revised by W.R. JENKINS. Drainage & Sanitation   Batsford 1936

✳ Dept. of Environment. Refuse Disposal £1.75p   H.M.S.O. 1971

  GARNER, J.F. The Law of Public Cleansing   Shaw & Sons 1965
                The Law of Sewers & Drains

✳ GOTAAS, H.B. Composting (sanitary disposal & reclammation of
                         organic wastes) monograph series No. 31   W.H.O. 1956

  IMHOFF, K. MULLER W.J. & THISTLE THWAYTE D.K.B.
                Disposal of sewage & other water borne wastes   London 1956

✳ KIRA A. The Bathroom

  Military Engineering. Min. of Defence.
       Vol Vll Accommodation & Installation,.
       Part 1X Expeditionary Force Depots 1953 (57—595—0—53) 15/—
       Part X Sewage & Sullage Disposal Works. Sewage Pumping Stations.
               Standard Designs. August 19th 1944. 7/6

  Min of Housing & Local Government.
       Memo. on Principles of Design for smal l domestic sewage treatment
       works. 9p H.M.S.O. '50's.?
✳ Min. of Housing & Local Government (Welsh Office)
       Taken for Granted. A Report on the Working Party on Sewage Disposal
       50p H.M.S.O. 1970

Info Area 10 <u>Waste Not</u>

Min. of Environment. <u>Small Sewage Works Operators Handbook.</u> 17½p   H.M.S.O. 1965

MACDONALD O.J.S. <u>Small Sewage Disposal Systems</u>   London 1952

SALE, C. <u>The Specialist.</u>   Putnam 1956

✳ WAGNER, E.G. & LANOIX J.N. <u>Excreta Disposal for Rural Areas and Small</u>
                               <u>Communities</u> mono. series No. 39 $5   W.H.O.1958

W.H.O. <u>Guide to Hygiene & Sanitation in Aviation.</u>   W.H.O.1960
        <u>Treatment and Disposal of Wastes</u>   " 1967
        <u>Tech. report series No. 367</u>
        <u>Design & Operation of Septic Tanks</u> mono series 18   " 1953

WRIGHT, L. <u>Clean & Decent. A fascinating history of the bathroom & toilet</u> R.K.P 1960

UNGEWITTER, C ed. <u>Science & Salvage</u>   Crosby Lockwood & Son Ltd 1944

INFO AREA 11 <u>SOURCE</u> – useful addresses etc.

Royal Horticultural Society, Vincent Square, London S.W.1. (excellent library)

<u>Seedsmen specialising in unusual vegetables and herbs</u>

KATHLEEN HUNTER, Wheal Francis, Callestick, Truro, Cornwall

GEORGE BUNYARD, Maidstone, Kent.

THE HERB FARM, Seal, Sevenoaks, Kent.

CARTERS TESTED SEEDS, Raynes Park, London S.W.20

<u>Well boring Equipment</u>

Kenmore Engineering, Dickinson Place, South Berstead Industrial Estate, Bognor Regis.

<u>The National Agricultural Advisory Service</u>

The Vegetarian Society, 53 Marloes Road, London W.8.

British Beekeepers Association, 55 Chipstead Lane, Riverhead, Sevenoaks, Kent.

Museum of English Rural Life, The University, White Knights Park, Reading.

Dried Foods – SWELS FOODS (EM), Crowle nr. Scunthorpe, Lincs.

Food Synthesis, Rothamstead Experimental Station, England. (nr. Harpenden, HERTS.)

Modern composting toilet and waste system. – Rikard Lindstroem, AB Clivus,
                                              Tonstigen 6, S–135 00 Tyresoe,
                                              SWEDEN

Urban Growth – contact Dave Harrison, 01 405 1576

Glass House Crops Research Institute, Rustington, Littlehampton, Sussex.

Rudolph Steiner House, 35 Park Road, London N.W.1.

Nature Conservancy, 19 Belgrave Square, London S.W.1.

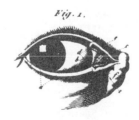

Fig. 1.

BIBLIOGRAPHY EIGHT